"In *The Path to a Livable Future*, Stan Cox shows how Covid, climate change, and racism have common roots in violation of planetary boundaries, ecological limits, and the rights of all people to justice and equality. He warns us that technological fixes in medicine, agriculture, and energy will deepen the crises. Above all, he shows that a healthy, just, sustainable future is possible if we reduce our ecological footprint and share the earth's gifts equitably. For this we need to organize, resist, imagine, and forge another path together."
—Vandana Shiva, author of *Who Really Feeds the World?: The Failures of Agribusiness and the Promise of Agroecology*

"As Cox shows in this devastating but clear-eyed assessment, the multiple existential crises of our modern world—from climate change to pandemics—are interrelated and can be traced back to centuries of colonial domination of land and people. Unfettered capitalism is the through-line that ties it all together, and it is only through degrowth, anti-racism, and anti-colonialism that a sustainable and just future can be imagined."
—Dina Gilio-Whitaker, author of *As Long as Grass Grows: The Indigenous Fight for Environmental Justice from Colonization to Standing Rock*

"Stan Cox stands in a class of his own. Chronicling the emergence of a translocal alliance including Black, Indigenous and people of color, and a growing number of white folks outside urban centers who have started coming to terms with the pervasive coloniality of our agrarian system and political institutions, *The Path to a Livable Future* is a testament to the fact that meaningful responses to the multifarious crises we face are unlikely to come—first and foremost—from traditional urban liberal strongholds. Having masterfully demonstrated in *Any Way You Slice It* and *The Green New Deal and Beyond* that climate breakdown was fundamentally an energy-rationing and wealth-redistribution issue, Cox continues to meticulously lay the groundwork for the radical paradigm shift that the ecosphere, our politics, and our economics so urgently require."

—Felix Marquardt, author of *The New Nomads: How the Migration Revolution Is Transforming Our Lives for the Better*

"When it comes to the climate crisis, our governments are still in complete denial about the scale of what needs to be done. Stan Cox cuts through the fog of mediocrity and offers a clear, honest vision for how social movements can win a truly just and sustainable society. There are few books I would recommend as wholeheartedly as this one. Don't miss it."

—Jason Hickel, author of *Less Is More: How Degrowth Will Save the World*

"*The Path* shows us that the calamitous problems faced by all humanity, from pandemic to environmental devastation and settler colonialism, have a common root: the Western doctrine of looting and exploitation. Cox lays out a refreshingly grounded roadmap for the survival of all life on earth, based on up-to-date science, and anchored in the racial justice imperative. Global civilization is on a disastrous trajectory that can only be averted through holistic and bold pivots. *The Path* charts the way forward and gives us a reason to cling to hope."

—Leah Penniman, co-founder of Soul Fire Farm, author of *Farming While Black: Soul Fire Farm's Practical Guide to Liberation on the Land*

THE PATH TO A LIVABLE FUTURE

THE PATH TO A
LIVABLE FUTURE

A New Politics to Fight Climate Change, Racism,
and the Next Pandemic

STAN COX

FOREWORD BY ZENOBIA JEFFRIES WARFIELD

CITY LIGHTS BOOKS | Open Media Series

Open Media Series Editor: Greg Ruggiero
Cover design: Victor Mingovits

ISBN: 978-0-87286-878-6
eISBN: 978-0-87286-856-4

Library of Congress Cataloging-in-Publication Data

Names: Cox, Stan, author.
Title: The path to a livable future : a new politics to fight climate
    change, racism, and the next pandemic / Stan Cox ; foreword by Zenobia
    Jeffries Warfield.
Description: San Francisco : City Lights Books, [2021] | Series: Open Media
    Series | Includes bibliographical references.
Identifiers: LCCN 2021018340 | ISBN 9780872868786 (Trade Paperback)
Subjects: LCSH: Environmentalism—United States. | Environmental
    policy—United States. | Racism—United States. | Public health—United
    States. | Food industry and trade—Government policy—United States.
Classification: LCC GE197 .C485 2021 | DDC 304.20973—dc23
LC record available at https://lccn.loc.gov/2021018340

City Lights Books are published at the City Lights Bookstore
261 Columbus Avenue, San Francisco, CA 94133
www.citylights.com

CONTENTS

THE PATH TO A LIVABLE FUTURE

FOREWORD

THE INVITATION TO write the foreword for Stan Cox's *The Path to a Livable Future: A New Politics to Fight Climate Change, Racism, and the Next Pandemic*, included a quote from my introduction to YES! Magazine's Spring 2021 issue on ecological civilization: "Stan's vision, like yours, is centered on the premise that 'The path toward an ecological civilization moves us from an uncivilized society based on selfish wealth accumulation to one that is community-oriented and life-affirming.'"

I remember the day I wrote that. It was not long after the insurrection at the U.S. Capitol. I was incensed by so many white people's response to what happened. "This is not America," they said. "This *is* America," I responded in a published commentary.

I challenged those reading my words to do better—to create a better world. If they really believed that the mob violence we witnessed was un-American behavior, they should prove it. Protest, organize, mobilize against harmful policies and ideologies that continue to oppress Black, Indigenous, Brown, Latino, and Asian people, those who've been systemically marginalized in this country and in many cases cast away. Resist politicians and social formations that support imperialist, white supremacist, capitalist, patriarchal ideologies that perpetuate injustice and deny that our consumption habits directly impact global warming.

That's just a start.

1

And still, as I wrote my introduction to that YES! issue, I was simultaneously feeling hopeful, encouraged by the stories we'd put together in that issue. "Progress toward an ecological civilization is already in motion.... *We're on our way.*"

It is a message that I wholeheartedly believe, despite a global pandemic, economic devastation, climate disasters, environmental injustices, racial inequities, global uprisings, and continued state and community violence. Even with many people simply going back to business as usual—eager to forget the world has lost millions of people to COVID-19 and that millions more are still infected—yes, I still believe!

My understanding of what an ecological civilization is did not come without challenges. I was dismayed to find that the majority of the people writing about this "new" way forward were mostly of the same race and gender as those who created the current dysfunctional civilization of separation, exploitation, extraction, and violence: white and male. Yet many of the ideas and solutions percolating have Indigenous and female roots—whether in the Americas, Africa, or Asia. Centering Black, Brown, Indigenous, and Asian perspectives became crucial. As I edited the ecological civilization issue, I found that the work now being given a new framing *was in fact already being done,* mostly at a grassroots level, and in some cases for centuries.

Stan Cox's *The Path to a Livable Future* offers a blueprint for the work necessary to build such a future. He shows how to do it—and quickly—by organizing social movements to fight together for the common good. Importantly, he centers historically marginalized Black, Brown, and Indigenous perspectives and their roles. "De-marginalization," he writes, "involves not just addressing matters of racial and environmental injustice, but centralizing the organizing roles of communities of color in the collective process of creating the governance necessary for a dignified and livable future for all."

As an institution, *YES!* is constantly exploring how we human beings can live equitably and without hoarding and impoverishment. There is enough for every being: enough food, enough water, enough land to steward, enough shelter, enough love, enough rest, enough work, enough income. *Enough for all to thrive.* Our Fall 2021 issue, with a lead article from Stan, addresses the question: *What is Enough?* We will continue to ask difficult questions, and seek solutions that develop a future that is open, inclusive, and life-affirming.

From food access, energy rationing, land use, workers' rights, racism, pandemics, and environmental injustice, and climate disasters, Stan describes a political restructuring of our systems in his "to do list for the 2020s." It includes nationalization and a rapid phase-out of fossil fuels; allocating resources for meeting essential needs; democratically run public utilities; participatory budgeting of both public funds and energy resources; fair-shares energy rationing; global climate justice; an overhaul of our food system; and expansion of long-standing mutual aid and environmental justice movements that have always been essential in the struggle to demarginalize communities. Regarding mutual aid efforts as part of deep systemic change, Stan draws inspiration from Huey Newton of the Black Panthers, who said, "That is why we call them survival programs, meaning *survival pending revolution.*"

None of these are new solutions. And that's a point Stan emphasizes. What would be "new" is our collective approach for ecological transformation and centering the leadership of communities most impacted by systemic racism, inequity, state violence, environmental injustice, and global pandemics.

And now we're paying attention.

COVID-19 captured our collective attention. At one point, people were referring to it as the great equalizer. Those who didn't already know, soon learned that this was a false narrative. The number of cases and deaths revealed quickly that communities of color were disproportionately ravaged by the virus.

Familiar regions succumbing to wildfires in the United States and Australia, and a snowstorm crippling Texas, also captured our collective attention—though not the ongoing water crisis in Jackson, Mississippi; I don't have to guess why that is. And finally, state violence against Black people captured our collective attention. We not only witnessed the May 25, 2020 killing of George Floyd, but felt the breath leave his body as convicted murderer Derek Chauvin, a former Minneapolis police officer, pressed his knee onto Floyd's neck for over nine minutes.

That was the first time in my lifetime that I saw white people in numbers in the streets protesting for Black people—all around the country and around the world. It seemed like a tipping point had been reached and the tide was finally turning. White Americans were finally listening…finally responding to the historical violence and inequities plaguing the rest of the nation.

But are they still listening?

Stan says the answer had better be *yes*. The failure to listen is what got us here in the first place.

In the pages ahead, Stan reminds us that there will be no vaccine to immunize ourselves against racism and economic marginalization; there will be no quick shot we can take to prevent the mass extinctions, wildfires, drought, and food-chain collapse that climate scientists forecast for us if we do not act now. Resistance and organizing are the vaccine. *We are the vaccine.*

The path to a livable future exists, but we must consciously choose to take it. It takes asking difficult questions, a willingness to listen, and a commitment to act together for the benefit of all. Let's be positive, and forge ahead, however uneasy and unsure we may be. Onward, *together*.

ZENOBIA JEFFRIES WARFIELD
EXECUTIVE EDITOR, *YES! MAGAZINE*

INTRODUCTION

T HROUGHOUT THE AFTERNOON and evening of November 7, 2020, my family, my friends, and I could not take our eyes off the spontaneous street celebrations that had erupted outside the White House and in cities across the country. Hearing that Joe Biden and Kamala Harris were projected to win Pennsylvania's electoral votes, throngs came out to celebrate the demise of the Trump presidency. Watching the revelry in Times Square on TV, my mind went straight to the iconic photographs of crowds celebrating on the same spot seventy-five years earlier when Nazi Germany was finally defeated in Europe. The street party back then marked the end of a terrible struggle and the certainty of better days ahead; this time, the joyous eruptions provided only a brief moment of respite from years of fear and cruelty endured during Trump's presidency. The next morning, it would be back to the Covid-19 pandemic and the fights against authoritarianism, white supremacy, and ecological breakdown—struggles that continue to become more urgent with each passing day.

Much effort has gone into drawing lessons from the year 2020, some of them grim, others inspiring. Yet in my view, we collectively have failed to accept the most urgent messages that were delivered to us by that terrible year. There were acknowledgments here and there that the widely expressed desire to "get back to normal" was not going to be either possible or adequate. The Biden/Harris campaign slogan "Build Back Better" implied improvement. However, given the realities we continue to face—a global ecological emergency, a public health system in tatters, economic apartheid, persistent assaults on civil rights and democracy—a better normal is insufficient and unacceptable.

As Trump's presidency finally lurched to an end, excitement and support for climate action surged. In particular, the possibility of an industrial mobilization for wind and solar energy rebounded, echoing the enthusiasm that had swirled around the plan for a Green New Deal in 2018–2019. In that pre-pandemic period, with unemployment well below 4 percent, the plan's proponents had emphasized economic stimulus only in passing. As death tolls and jobless rates soared and wildfires raged, however, many writers, ranging from liberals to democratic socialists, promoted a "green," pro-growth industrial policy as a central element in restoring livelihoods and income lost during the pandemic.

Big public spending was indeed badly needed to relieve the economic misery being suffered by millions. But the policy was also intended to revive the pre-pandemic drive for growth in production, consumption, and wealth accumulation. That drive has always been prioritized over mitigating the ecological degradation, racism, and injustice perpetrated by a political economy centered on the relentless pursuit of profit. In 2020, those disasters were having by far their cruelest impacts on Indigenous, Black, and Latino people—the same communities historically denied a voice in the decision-making process. The path to a livable future now involves not just reforming an unjust system, or budgeting a little more here and there to "underserved" communities, but abolishing marginalization itself. By co-creating movements from all sectors of society, we organize in ways that are inclusive, open, democratic, and diverse. This is how we become unstoppable, and how we seed our present struggles with the dignified future we collectively envision.

In my previous book, *The Green New Deal and Beyond*, I focused tightly on the climate emergency and national public policies that will be necessary to end it. In this book, which zooms out to a wide-angle view of an entire society in rapid flux, I look to the movements now demanding the kind of transformation that's necessary to get us all through the multiple, entangled emergencies that finally captured the nation's attention in 2020. Has white America at long last started listening to the rest of the country? The answer had better be yes, because four hundred years of white settler-colonialism—and the failure to pay heed to Indigenous, Black, and Latino examples of a better way—have created the calamities we now face, including ecological destabilization.

Climate impacts are already being felt, and not uniformly. Corina Newsome, a wildlife conservationist at Georgia Southern University, told the *Washington Post*, "Climate change is the most immediate threat for the marginalized people of this country and of the world.... But that also means we are the most quick to act." For example, a *Post* poll found that "at least twice as many black and Hispanic teens participated in school walkouts on climate change than their white counterparts; they were also more likely to say people need to take action in the next year or two."[1] De-marginalization involves not just addressing matters of racial and environmental injustice, but centralizing the organizing roles of communities of color in the collective process of creating the governance necessary for a dignified and livable future for all.

In early 2021, Nick Estes, an assistant professor of American Studies at the University of New Mexico and citizen of the Lower Brule Sioux Tribe, cited some encouraging developments under the new administration in Washington—the end of the Keystone XL pipeline, a moratorium on oil and gas leases in the Arctic national wildlife refuge, and restoration of protections for Indigenous sacred sites. "None of these victories would have been possible," wrote Estes, "without sustained Indigenous resistance and tireless advocacy....'Green' techno fixes and consumer-based solutions might provide short-term answers, but they don't stop the plunder of Native lands."[2] The economic and environmental policies now being looked to for a post-pandemic society are heavy on the techno-fixes and every bit as inadequate as those that were promoted before 2020; in fact, they are even weaker, relative to the crises at hand. Without sweeping grassroots action, the forces that pushed us into the multiple crises of 2020—unshakable faith in technology and markets, the compulsion to exploit ecosystems, a belief in growth without limits—will be relied upon in a vain quest to "build back better," to restore the ecologically reckless U.S. that existed before 2020, only this time with more and better jobs, and without a would-be tyrant in the White House. Yes, we need good jobs for all, but building solar and wind power plants and producing electric cars will not end the climate emergency. We have reached a stage in which the pre-pandemic model of normal is not only unsustainable; it's no longer survivable. In particular, the time has come for the institutions that have dominated environmental policy for a half century to yield right-of-way. Michelle Martinez, the acting executive director of the Michigan Environmental Justice Coalition, told *Politico* in 2020, "The environmental movement was born of a colonial narrative, that nature was out there to be explored and to be used....I've had people at mainstream environmental organizations tell me point blank, 'If we start doing this racial justice stuff, we're going to lose some of our funders.' And that risk is real. It's this idea that focusing on racial justice, it becomes less about the environment. And that's simply not true. That's that colonial mindset."[3]

That the pandemic exposed vulnerabilities in our health care, food, and transportation systems was obvious; how to make those systems more robust and adaptable was less apparent. Disparate responses to the pandemic also illuminated and exacerbated the exploitation of

Black, Latino, and Indigenous communities and workers, while further whipping up the white supremacism that Donald Trump had been stoking over the previous four years. When the broad-based Black Lives Matter–led uprising against the police war on Black people swept the nation and world in 2020, it inspired all of the nation's movements for justice and sustainability, providing a road map for the way forward. During the Minneapolis protests that followed George Floyd's killing, activist Tamika Mallory delivered an electrifying speech in which she said, "This is a coordinated activity happening across this nation, and so we are in a state of emergency....America has looted black people. America looted the Native Americans when they first came here; looting is what you do."[4]

Mallory's message applies even more broadly. In addition to stealing the land and enslaving people to farm it, white settler-colonists plundered and violated the land itself, wreaking havoc upon the interconnected system of soils, waters, habitats, and atmosphere of the continent. One result of this relentless assault has been severe erosion not only of soil but also of health and quality of life in marginalized communities, both urban and rural. This erosion became increasingly clear through the uneven manner Covid has impacted communities of color.

Racial, economic, and environmental justice issues thus emerged from 2020 even more deeply entangled than they were before. Debates over when to declare that workers and the goods and services they produce are "essential" were more about profit and prejudice than about ensuring supplies of basic necessities. The "essential" designation resulted in the increased exploitation of already exploited workers and communities on the one hand, and favoritism toward ecologically destructive businesses that cater to the affluent on the other. In this book, I argue not only for an end to labor exploitation and systemic racism but also for a more serious discussion of the hard collective decisions that must be made regarding which goods and services must be produced and which should not be produced at all.

At one point in writing *The Green New Deal and Beyond*, I made an argument for what might be called consumers' climate strikes, asking readers in part to "imagine the impact of audacious mass boycotts of air travel, or house and car buying." In early 2020, as I was making final edits on the manuscript and rereading those words, I thought, "Yeah, right, what are the chances *that's* going to happen, ha, ha?" But at that very moment, as I sat there shaking my head, news reports were emerging of a highly contagious respiratory disease hitting Wuhan, China. Within weeks, the unthinkable was happening. Air travel dropped 95 percent; the world's passenger aircraft fleet was almost completely grounded. Human civilization survived a halt in air travel—but now it is once again threatened by its resumption.

Ongoing emergencies in racial justice, climate, and public health jointly present us with grave challenges throughout society. In the pages ahead, I focus on three interconnected sectors of the economy where they converge in many ways: energy, land use, and food. The roots of the crises that collided in 2020, and the heavy impacts they will have on our future, are so intimately interwoven that these problems must all be resolved together, or they will never be resolved. Accordingly, it was clear to me they could not be dealt with individually, each in its own chapter. I therefore decided to work through the various entangled roots all at once, weighing the actions that are necessary to win a dignified and sustainable future for all, and seeking viable ways to overcome the material and political obstacles to such actions.

"How do we transform ourselves and one another," asks Black Lives Matter cofounder, Alicia Garza, "into the fighters we need to be to win and keep winning?" Joining the nationwide revolt against systemic racism, including marching and rallying with my fellow residents of Salina, Kansas, brought me new optimism and answers. The confrontation with systemic racism that erupted in 2020, reaching even as far as little Salina, has created multiple openings.

Widening them, however, is only the beginning, and navigating the rough terrain on the other side will require a lot of improvisation and perseverance.

The terrain ahead started looking rougher than ever on January 6, 2021, when a violent white mob stormed the U.S. Capitol with the aim of nullifying the outcome of the presidential election. Afterward, the *Guardian* noted that the insurrection was far from the first of its type: "Mobs of white Americans unwilling to accept multiracial democracy have successfully overturned or stolen elections before: in Wilmington, North Carolina, in 1898, in Colfax, Louisiana, in 1873 and New Orleans in 1874, and, in Hamburg, South Carolina" in 1876.[5] By repeatedly attacking the institutions responsible for enforcing racial justice after the Civil War, such violent mobs managed to shut down Reconstruction after barely a decade, thereby maintaining white supremacy as the law of the land for another nine decades. The Capitol insurrection failed, at least in its immediate goal. But the assault on multiracial democracy is as serious as it was in the 1870s, and far from over.

In the tumultuous fall of 2020, Angela Davis observed, "So many struggles have been about bringing the marginalized into the fold of the democracy, and that is where we make many mistakes. W.E.B. DuBois argued that democracy could not remain the same and respond to the needs of those who had been previously enslaved. The democracy itself would have to be transformed, and new institutions would have to be created....We are now preparing to do work which should have happened over 150 years ago."[6]

There is much work to be done to win a livable future, and no time left for dawdling.

1.

THE CRUELEST YEAR

The excluded begin to realize, having endured everything, that they can endure everything. They do not know the precise shape of the future, but they know that the future belongs to them. They realize this—paradoxically—by the failure of the moral energy of their oppressors and begin, almost instinctively, to forge a new morality, to create the principles on which a new world will be built.

—James Baldwin, *No Name in the Street*, 1972[7]

VOTING DONALD TRUMP out of the White House may have forestalled a descent into fascism, but it did not resolve our national predicament. It's as if, like Leonardo DiCaprio's character in the 2015 film *The Revenant*, we had fought off a bear attack, but we were all still lost in the wilderness, gravely injured and not knowing how many more bears were out there. The election results preserved an opportunity to reverse the climate emergency, but achieving that with the necessary speed is now an even more daunting prospect, given that we lost four precious years. Trump's defeat most likely prevented many thousands more Covid-19 deaths, but it came too late to save the hundreds of thousands of lives that could have been saved. And while freeing ourselves from white supremacy at the highest levels of the Executive Branch achieved an important victory, even more strenuous efforts lie ahead to completely emancipate U.S. society from racial injustice.

We lived to fight another day, but we didn't buy ourselves any time. The urgency of our predicament is even greater than before the nightmare of 2020 began. Not only does the death toll from police shootings of Black people keep rising, communities of color remain outside many of the political processes required to restructure the institutions that directly impact their security, safety, health, and quality of life. Millions of people don't have access to adequate food, health care, or clean air and water. And we are hurtling faster than ever toward the deadline for ending greenhouse emissions. The United Nations reported in 2020 that a decade of global procrastination on climate has dramatically raised the bar for effective climate mitigation. Greenhouse emissions will now need to be reduced at *four times* the annual rate that would have been required if serious collective climate action had started *in 2010*.[8] That will be exceedingly difficult, but there's still a chance. Procrastinate a little longer, and our chance of success dwindles significantly.

For decades, but especially since the Hurricane Katrina disaster of 2005, there has been much speculation over the threshold for declaring and acting on the global ecological emergency—in other words, how big and extreme do climate disasters have to be, how many lives do they have to take, how high must the price in economic misery be, before our society collectively decides to do what is necessary? Disasters have become more deadly, more destructive, and more numerous, but they have not yet reached the threshold at which our society is willing to shake off its resistance to change. We now need to educate ourselves to understand that the disasters we face are part of an ongoing process, a trajectory of calamities increasing in momentum and intensity, and not a series of unrelated one-offs. To wait until a disaster is massive enough to incentivize collective change may very well mean to wait far too long, as there will be no vaccine to immunize ourselves against the mass extinctions, wildfires, drought, and food chain collapse that climate scientists forecast for us. The time to act is now.

CONFRONT EVERYTHING AT ONCE

PUBLIC HEALTH AND climatic stability are linked and must be dealt with together. Likewise, without a focus on abolishing injustice, working on climate change alone will address only the symptoms, not the root structural causes of our collective maladies. In some ways, the onset of the Covid-19 pandemic delayed and complicated efforts to tackle the global climate emergency. In other ways, it provided a glimpse of what decisive action on the global ecological crisis should look like—and what it should not look like. Many of the same ecologically sound measures that can reduce risk of future pandemics are also necessary to prevent climatic catastrophe.

Necessarily bold climate action has long been rejected because it is seen as an obstacle to unlimited economic growth, and thus too extreme to be considered by a capitalist political system. The pandemic woke us to the fact that a five-alarm global emergency requires that we set aside business as usual in order to take extraordinary actions and accept dramatic departures from everyday life. Some nations did that in 2020, but unfortunately, neither the U.S. government nor the owning and investing classes had the stomach for extraordinary measures. Throughout the year, neither the coronavirus nor the climate emergency was adequately addressed.

The full story of 2020, however, was even bigger. The pandemic and economic collapse not only converged with the climatic nightmares of the wildfires in the West and the onrush of hurricanes and tropical storms that depleted the weather authorities' alphabetical list of twenty-six planned names and then ran nine letters deep into the Greek alphabet—it also coincided with America's racial reckoning and broad support of the Black Lives Matter groundswell; with a street-level struggle against white supremacy and state violence; and with the battle to defend voting rights and the rule of law against the proto-fascist forces that were being mobilized by Team Trump through the Executive Branch. Peering back through that maelstrom, is it possible to discern both the necessity and the possibility of bottom-up transformation?

Exploitation of ecosystems and mineral resources is a triple threat, lying at the root of the climate emergency, the growing threat of pandemic diseases, and the widespread degradation of the environmental circumstances in which marginalized communities are often stuck. The threats to the climate, public health, and local environments have a disproportionate impact on people of color, Indigenous communities, immigrants, and other marginalized people, both in the United States and across the globe. Consequences include poverty, hunger, illness, and oppression. These political legacies of white supremacy continue to undermine our collective well-being. The national failure to act on the climate emergency has its roots in an attitude held by much of affluent white society that its members can shield themselves while marginalized and impoverished people here and around the world suffer the worst consequences of deadly heat waves, flooding, landslides, and storms. Countering white, male, and other supremacies at the root of environmental injustice requires diversifying the process of change itself to weave in the strategies, leadership, social dynamics, and traditions of communities of color, Indigenous communities, women and youth, and others whose voices have not yet been heard.

Cruel calculation also lies behind the failure of many of our political leaders and their supporters to deal effectively with the health injustices that were exacerbated by the Covid-19 pandemic.

Throughout 2020, the coronavirus killed people in Black, Indigenous, and Latino communities at approximately double the rate suffered by white people. In 2020, life expectancy decreased by nine months in the U.S. white population, by almost two years in the Latino population, and by 2.7 years in the Black population. When vaccines finally became available, their rates of delivery reflected a perverse logic, one not of medical ethics but of privilege. By mid-February 2021, 9.1 percent of whites had received at least the first dose, compared with 4.5 percent of Blacks and 3.5 percent of Latinos. Waiting at the tail end of the queue to obtain vaccinations were the nation's 3 million farmworkers, for all the same reasons that they'd had so little access to protective equipment and occupational measures to prevent infection throughout the pandemic. In one bright spot, Indigenous people, who have suffered higher Covid-19 death rates than any other group, had the highest inoculation rate: 11.6 percent. This success came thanks in part to tribal vaccination programs that were apparently "running more efficiently and effectively than in many states," according to the *Guardian*, as well as greater acceptance of vaccines than prevails in non-Indigenous communities.[9]

White decisionmakers on the right could look at the racial and ethnic differences in death rates and conveniently see the strange new coronavirus as someone else's problem. They remained as unconcerned about the white privilege and systemic racism that created the huge disparities in the virus's impact as they were about the virus itself. With economic growth at stake, those near the peak of the wealth pyramid seemed to view the pandemic, like the climate emergency, as something against which their wealth was a shield, protecting them until business as usual could properly resume. That kind of thinking would have catastrophic consequences.

In 2020, it became crystal clear that American society could not resolve its proliferating crises one by one. Public health officials were constantly featured in the media saying that Washington couldn't revive the economy until the pandemic was suppressed. But it was also impossible to deal with either Covid-19 or the climate emergency without confronting systemic racism head-on. To quote the climate activist Vanessa Nakate, "Every climate activist should be advocating for racial justice because if your climate justice does not involve the most affected communities, then it is not justice at all."[10] Furthermore, neither newly emerging pandemic pathogens nor runaway greenhouse warming can be avoided without reversing ecological destruction. And, to complete the circle, neither racial justice nor health justice nor environmental justice nor climate justice can be fully secured without turning the existing economy inside out, dedicating it to meeting society's needs, not feeding the net worth of the plutocrats. Sacoby Wilson, a University of Maryland environmental health scientist, put it this way: "Covid-19 has shown that we have a lot of Haves in this country, but we have a lot more Have-Nots. Our policies have disproportionally benefited the Haves while disproportionately impacting the Have-Nots. To address the disparities in Covid-19, we have to address our structural inequalities in this country. The first place to start is race and racism."[11]

UNTIL ALL OF US ARE FREE

ON MAY 25, 2020, Derek Chauvin and three other Minneapolis police officers murdered George Floyd. In the six years that had passed between the police killing of Michael Brown in Ferguson, Missouri, and Floyd's death, people in the United States had witnessed countless video recordings of unarmed Black people being killed by police, and the Black Lives Matter movement had kept the issue prominent in the news. But the sight of Chauvin kneeling on the neck of his handcuffed victim for more than nine minutes, and the sound of Floyd's words as he was being killed—"Please man...I can't breathe...I can't breathe...Please...Mama...Mama...I'm through... I'm through...I can't breathe, officer...Don't kill me"—broke through as other news and images had not. People in Minneapolis and in towns and cities across the country rose up in grief and indignation. The weeks of protest were said to be the largest street demonstrations in the nation's history, with as many as 26 million taking part. On June 6, 2020, half a million people turned out in approximately 550 places nationwide.[12] On June 20, workers in 160 cities took part in a Strike for Black Lives.

"It was the well-prepared founders of Black Lives Matter, including Californians Alicia Garza, Patrisse Cullors and Opal Tometi, who are most responsible for turning what could have merely been a moment of rage into a months-long movement," wrote Erika D. Smith in the *Los Angeles Times*.[13] The protests were the most racially diverse yet seen in the U.S., and a large majority of the general public supported both those protests and the broader Black Lives Matter movement. When local police, far-right militiamen, and Trump's grab-bag of anonymous, menacing federal lawmen responded to nonviolent protests with excessive violence, the uprising only gained strength. Comparing that moment to the decade of efforts to secure full citizenship and rights for freed Black people that followed the Civil War, *The Atlantic*'s Adam Serwer is calling for a "New Reconstruction" in the 2020s:

> The urgency of addressing this crisis has been under-
> scored by the ongoing behavior of police departments,
> whose officers have reacted much as the white South did
> after Appomattox: by brutalizing the people demanding
> change....Yet the more the police sought to violently repress
> the protesters, the more people spilled into the streets in
> defiance, risking a solitary death in a hospital bed in order
> to assert their right to exist, to not have their lives stolen by
> armed agents of the state....At the height of Reconstruction,
> racist horrors produced the political will to embrace mea-
> sures once considered impossibly idealistic, such as Black

male suffrage. Many Black Lives Matter activists have a similarly radical vision.[14]

As Serwer notes, millions of people of all colors and ages took part in the protests despite the expectation that they might face an increased risk of coronavirus infection. Donald Trump and other supporters of the killer cops tried to exploit the protests by calling for even harsher "law and order" measures. They even charged Trump's opponents with trying to hurt his electoral chances by calling his in-person rallies "superspreading events" but at the same time taking to the streets in large numbers themselves when they saw a chance to hurt him politically. This was claptrap. Protesters, mostly masked, marched and rallied outdoors, keeping as much distance among themselves as they could manage. Collectively and individually, they (we) felt compelled to support a historic turning point in the long struggle for racial justice, and took action to lower everyone's risk as much as possible. And it worked. A National Bureau of Economic Research analysis found that weeks after the height of the protests, there was no evidence that the events had increased the numbers of Covid-19 cases in U.S. cities.[15] If anyone was being cynical, it was Trump and staff for producing campaign rallies with tightly packed crowds of maskless followers who screamed and chanted throughout. Those spectacles became a kind of propaganda in the cultural battle over Covid-19. And they did boost the spread of the virus, which eventually reached the First Family itself when Donald, Melania, and Barron Trump all became infected. A Stanford University study estimated that the Trump rallies held between late June and late September collectively led to 30,000 new coronavirus infections that resulted in as many as seven hundred deaths.[16]

Meanwhile, Black lives continued not to matter to law enforcement. CBS News documented that in the five months leading up to Floyd's death, 105 Black people were killed by police, and in the three months that followed his murder, another fifty-nine were killed. In

2020, a Black person was more than three times as likely to suffer death at the hands of police as a white person. By the end of that summer, the American Medical Association, the American College of Emergency Physicians, the American Psychological Association, and seventy local governments had passed resolutions declaring institutional racism a public health crisis. Activists and experts told *YES!* magazine that the resolutions should be followed up with action, starting with not providing funds for police to respond to nonviolent situations, such as checking on physical wellness or incidents in which people are suffering from mental health or substance abuse problems—situations better handled by other agencies.

The pandemic of white supremacy is old news to people of color; it has been taking lives since the first days of settler colonialism. As Roxanne Dunbar Ortiz points out in *An Indigenous History of the United States*, "The history of the United States is a history of settler colonialism—the founding of a state based on the ideology of white supremacy, the widespread practice of African slavery, and a policy of genocide and land theft." The consensual national narrative, says Dunbar Ortiz, is a myth that embraces atrocities on a massive scale. Acknowledging the realities of U.S. history—and their injurious legacies in the present—however, is a necessary step in de-normalizing the violence of white supremacy.

OUT OF THE FIRE, BACK INTO THE FRYING PAN

FOR A SOCIETY in great peril, the righteous eruption over police violence and overt racism reignited hope that even broader transformation could be demanded and achieved. The events of 2020 would reach into the underlying issues of systemic racism, including the geographical segregation that had persisted for almost six decades after the Civil Rights movement. The federal government's practice of marking off predominantly Black neighborhoods for purposes of denying home mortgage lending, a practice known as "redlining," was in effect from the 1930s to the 1960s, when it was finally banned by the Fair Housing Act. A half century after being opened to nondiscriminatory lending by the act, redlined neighborhoods have become more ethnically diverse, but the majority of residents continue to be people of color. And the impacts of redlining persist: residential segregation, with disparities in housing quality, public services, and local business activity; huge differences in average net worth between white families and Black and brown families, partly because of lower rates of home ownership by the latter; deep discrimination in education; and crucially, lack of access to good nutrition and public health services. The result, notes Leah Penniman, the cofounder of Soul Fire Farm in Petersburg, New York, is predictable: "Housing discrimination, through redlining, divestment in communities, urban renewal, gentrification, all of those systems...make your zip code one of the number one determiners of your life expectancy...often on race lines."[17]

Today, once-redlined neighborhoods are much more likely than others to have poorer air and water quality because of their proximity to power plants, dirty industrial development, or busy freight-hauling and transportation corridors. A 2019 study published in the Proceedings of the National Academy of Sciences arrived at an unambiguous conclusion: Particulate air pollution—the tiniest, deadliest particles of soot and ash, measuring less than 2.5 microns—"is disproportionately induced by the racial-ethnic majority and disproportionately inhaled by racial-ethnic minorities."[18] Because Black, Indigenous, and Latino communities buy and consume less, they are responsible for smaller quantities of dangerous particulate air pollutants than the country's overall average, but they are much more heavily exposed to such contamination, because communities of color are often situated in the most environmentally disadvantaged locations—near refineries, factories, incinerators, and so on.

Research published in the journal *Climate* in early 2020 found that the less visible threat posed by greenhouse warming is also greater in formerly redlined neighborhoods. There, people are more menaced by health problems and even death during heat waves than those living elsewhere, because they are surrounded by much more heat-trapping concrete and asphalt and far fewer trees or other vegetation. In a range of U.S. cities, redlined areas are five to twelve degrees hotter in summer than other residential areas in the same municipality. Once-redlined areas are also more vulnerable to flooding, because with so much impermeable surface, excess water can't percolate into the ground.[19]

Not surprisingly but tragically, these stressed neighborhoods faced a disproportionate health emergency as the pandemic spread and intensified. Their risk was raised by high-density living conditions; inadequate health care facilities; higher rates of police harassment, arrest, and detention; and lack of safe outdoor spaces. Furthermore, high levels of particulate air pollution dramatically elevate the risk of infection and severe illness with Covid-19. In a study published in the summer of 2020, a team of Italian researchers found a strong association between pollution levels and coronavirus infection and death rates. Ominously, they also found evidence that air pollution probably induces human lung cells to cover themselves with more ACE-2 receptors, which provide entry points for coronaviruses to invade.[20]

One factor more than any other raises risk of infection in marginalized communities: residents' occupations. Statistical analyses of mobility in low-, middle-, and high-income neighborhoods in the spring and early summer of 2020 found that travel from home to stores, restaurants, and other non-work destinations decreased uniformly, in accord with official restrictions. In contrast, commuting to workplaces decreased much less in low-income neighborhoods than in others, reflecting the fact that most low-wage essential jobs typically cannot be accomplished from home. These on-site jobs, which are disproportionately occupied by workers of color, create the greatest exposure to infectious disease.[21]

The threat posed by the one-two-three punch of greenhouse warming, airborne particulate matter, and the pandemic virus loomed large on the West Coast as wildfires raged out of control over an unprecedented land area. More than 4 million acres burned in California alone, doubling the acreage burned in the previous worst year. With the region's cities and towns blanketed in smoke, air quality sank to new lows, including in distressed urban areas where they were already chronically bad. The clouds of particles and toxins persisted for weeks. Those most threatened by the smoke, and therefore at elevated risk from Covid-19, were firefighters on the front lines. There too, health and climate disasters were compounded by injustice, when career firefighters earning solid salaries were joined in California by large numbers of prison inmates earning a dollar an hour in exchange for risking their lives and respiratory health.

As the pandemic's summer wave ripped through the Sunbelt, police carried on with shooting unarmed Black people, while local, state, and federal cops, sometimes seemingly allied with militia-style armed thugs, continued assaulting unarmed protesters of all races. The climate emergency, meanwhile, simmered on the back burner. For a short time, pandemic-induced lockdowns helped suppress greenhouse emissions and smog levels; thanks to the latter effect, urban dwellers were treated to bluer skies and longer views than they had seen in decades. During April 2020, with stay-at-home orders and business closures in place across much of the world, global carbon dioxide emissions derived from fossil fuels fell 17 percent below 2019 levels. But later, after months of rekindled economic activity, total 2020 emissions ended up just 9.2 percent below those of 2019—more realistically, fossil fuel emissions were 6.4 percent below, taking into account carbon from the year's record wildfire outbreaks. The dip in emissions had no effect on global atmospheric carbon dioxide concentrations, which continued to climb between July 2019 and July 2020.[22] The climate emergency, like the pandemic, did not "just one day go away," as Trump had predicted for the virus.

The most prominent rallying point for the climate movement remained the Green New Deal, still with nothing on paper more specific than a 2019 joint Congressional resolution. But the vision was crowded out of the news on most days. Rather than accelerating, the buildup of renewable energy capacity slowed as the pandemic and its economic fallout swept across the country. A recession-induced drop in electricity demand and falling fuel prices helped suppress investment in renewable energy. To make matters worse, disruption of supply chains for parts hindered the manufacturing of wind turbines and solar photovoltaic panels.

In July, with little fanfare, the Democratic Party's Biden-Sanders Unity Task Force released a platform-style report laying out the party's positions on health care, criminal justice and policing reform, climate, and other issues. Given top billing, the climate section declared national goals that included achieving net-zero greenhouse gas emissions for all new buildings by 2030; retrofitting a few million existing buildings; and achieving zero carbon and other pollution from power plants by 2035. The task force called for a federal Office of Climate Mobilization and pledged to "embed environmental justice and climate justice at the heart of our policy and governing agenda."[23] The report, however, proposed no explicit plan to eliminate greenhouse emissions or fossil-fuel burning, and it left the door wide open for nuclear energy. Like the Green New Deal, the Unity Task Force report relied on the erroneous assumption that an industrial mobilization to build up non-fossil energy capacity would automatically eliminate fossil fuels and other sources of greenhouse emissions.

Climate activists sounded the alarm when, just before the August party conventions, the Democratic National Committee mysteriously removed a plank from its campaign platform calling for an end to federal fossil-fuel subsidies. The Biden campaign stressed that, whatever the platform said, Biden would work to eliminate subsidies, but activists remained skeptical. Racial disparities in climatic and pollution impacts were reflected in polls showing that while fewer than half of white Americans were "alarmed" or "concerned" about climate change, 57 percent of Blacks and 70 percent of Latinos were alarmed or concerned.[24] Reverend Michael Malcom, the founder of the People's Justice Council, told the *Guardian*, "After I learned that they removed fossil fuel subsidies from the platform, whatever they said at that point kind of fell on skeptical ears. The communities that I represent, serve and work with—that is exactly what's killing us. It's also contributing heavily to climate change, but it's the subsidies that really harm black, brown, indigenous, poor communities....I really don't think they're looking at black life for real. The whole black life."[25]

Rev. Malcom's point—that a failure to confront systemic racism is a failure to confront the climate emergency, and vice versa—harmonized with a *Washington Post* op-ed that had been published a week after the killing of George Floyd. In the piece, Ayana Elizabeth Johnson wrote that she is a climate scientist, she's Black, and in her experience, racism and police violence were impeding efforts to eliminate America's outsize climate footprint. "I work on one existential crisis," she wrote, "but these days I can't concentrate because of another." Pointing to the poll showing Black people to be both more attentive to, and affected by, the climate emergency, she continued:

> Black people don't want to be protesting for our basic rights to live and breathe. We don't want to constantly justify our existence. Racism, injustice and police brutality are awful on their own, but are additionally pernicious because of the brain power and creative hours they steal from us. I think of one black friend of mine who wanted to be an astronomer, but gave up that dream because organizing for social justice was more pressing. Consider the discoveries not made, the

books not written, the ecosystems not protected, the art not created, the gardens not tended.[26]

Our outdated political/economic system has a rapid-fire way of throwing immediate crises at us, ones to which we cannot fail to respond, leaving us little time to confront long-term threats posed by the system itself that are just as urgent. This is true not only of the climate emergency, but also of the badly broken U.S. agriculture and food system.

THE FOOD WORKERS' PREDICAMENT

WITH THE PANDEMIC, many U.S. workers found themselves on the horns of a dilemma, with no say in its resolution. Laid-off workers had decreased risk of infection but were at increased risk of economic ruin and potential homelessness. Those who were declared essential kept their jobs and income but faced a higher probability of infection and illness, with few receiving sufficient compensation for putting their lives on the line. The Brookings Institution examined the wage policies that thirteen of the twenty largest retail corporations enacted in response to the pandemic. All of the companies had initiated policies for hazard pay in March, mostly in the form of small one-time or periodic bonuses and/ or temporary wage increases in the vicinity of $2 per hour. They didn't last long. By the end of June, three-fourths of the companies had already ended their wage increases and bonuses, and they did not resume them during the more serious coronavirus surges of the fall. "They stopped giving us the $2-an-hour hazard pay," a Safeway cashier told Brookings. "They gave us all a letter, as if to say, 'Coronavirus is over, you did it, you all are the real heroes, thank you for your service.' That is ridiculous—this is not over. We have not completed a tour of service and now things are safe. No, it is still dangerous....It is clear what the priority is: They don't want to pay us. Now they feel that they don't have to."[27] (Four companies—Target, Best Buy, Loews, and Home Depot—did much better, extending hazard pay through the rest of the year at least. Target and Best Buy ended up permanently raising their minimum wages to $15 per hour.)

The thirteen companies Brookings examined included some of the nation's largest grocery, pharmacy, home improvement, electronics, discount, and online retail giants. They were the chief providers of essential goods during year one of a pandemic when the nation was focusing on their products, and their profits rose accordingly—averaging an eye-popping 39 percent above 2019 profits. Of the extra $17 billion in total extra profit the thirteen raked in, almost two-thirds went to the two largest, Amazon and Walmart. Those two firms could have increased the hazard pay going to their essential workers *fourfold* and would still have piled up more profit than in 2019. Most of the companies instead plowed much of their new wealth into stock buybacks, which had the effect of increasing their market valuation. Brookings reported that, for example, "After ending its 'hero pay' in May, Kroger reported [in November] $211 million in stock buybacks in the second quarter, and announced a new $1 billion stock buyback program in September, sending stock prices up. Meanwhile, the company's frontline grocery workers have gone 181 days without hazard pay, and will enter this new, deadlier phase of the pandemic earning some of the lowest wages in the industry." At around the time Walmart sent its employees their final bonus check, the company announced a new $500 billion stock buyback—more than 40 percent as much money as the total hazard pay the company shelled out in 2020.[28]

Upstream from the big grocery and discount chains, workers in the nation's agricultural and food processing industries faced greater coronavirus risk while being compensated even more poorly. The pandemic exposed the fragility of the nation's farming and food-handling economy, as well as its injustices. Stark evidence came first out of the meatpacking industry, where workers were declared essential, thereby compelling them to labor in crowded, cold spaces that provide ideal conditions for the coronavirus to spread. In some plants, the virus infected 100 percent of the workforce. Soon, it became clear that the pandemic was ravaging not just meat and poultry plants but the entire food production and processing industry. Migrant farmworkers in fruit orchards and vegetable fields, disproportionately Latino, saw their infection rates soar as they worked to keep up with the panic buying that was overwhelming supermarkets. By summer, the Centers for Disease Control and Prevention (CDC) had issued guidelines for protecting farmworkers, but Trump's Labor Department chose not to enforce them, and most farm owners ignored the guidelines.

The virus spread quickly among the thousands of seasonal workers who arrive in southern New Jersey each year to harvest fruits and vegetables, sleep in cramped dormitories, and eat in crowded cafeterias. Farm managers who found that illness had left their operations shorthanded were allowed by the state to keep infected workers on the job; there was no paid sick leave. As with meatpacking, the novel coronavirus found other poorly ventilated, crowded, food-related facilities to be efficient incubators. It swept through a complex of hydroponic greenhouses in upstate New York. A single southern California city, Vernon, saw outbreaks in nine food facilities processing coffee, tea, frozen foods, deli meats, seaweed, baked goods, and other products. Yakima County, Washington, came to suffer the highest per-capita coronavirus infection rate on the West Coast. Fifty percent of the county's people are Latino, many of them working in agriculture and food. Seven hundred fruit-packing workers started walking out on strike in May over the lack of health safeguards. They soon reached settlements, with employers agreeing to provide personal protective equipment and follow CDC guidelines.

By the end of the year, more than a half million agricultural workers across the country had tested positive for the virus and at least 9,000 had died from it.[29] With physical distancing difficult in homes, transportation, and workplaces, these workers were especially vulnerable. To make matters worse, a justified fear of persecution by the Trump era's increasingly vicious immigration authorities deterred many workers from seeking medical care.

Laborers at a large pistachio farm in California's Central Valley went on strike when they learned that farm managers had not only failed to provide masks but had also hidden the fact that dozens of their co-workers had tested positive for the virus. In early summer, the town of Immokalee in southwest Florida, which is at the center of a large, intensive vegetable-growing area, had the highest infection rate of any zip code in the pandemic-wracked state. The virus continued to infect new human hosts in densely packed buses and vans that took workers to the fields and in their housing, which consisted mostly of mobile homes, each with numerous occupants.

Farm owners and managers generally resisted testing employees, contact tracing, education on health protection, and creating isolation areas for infected workers. Workers typically went maskless; on some farms, they were given masks and told to wear them only on days when state inspectors were coming. Farmworkers across the country were threatened with termination of employment if they complained about a lack of masks and gloves, or were ordered not to inform their fellow workers if they tested positive. A staff member with the Coalition of Immokalee Workers told the *Washington Post*, "We know that just about everyone we've confirmed [as Covid-19 positive] in Immokalee is in fact Indigenous, Mayan, or Latino, but they are listed as White."[30]

Some companies came up with devious strategies for keeping workers infection-free while they dodged their responsibility to offer health-protection measures such as paid sick leave, testing, and safer transportation. Lipman Family Farms, with tomato production in Virginia, South Carolina, and Florida, confined its workforce to the farm property, keeping people either in the field working or in and around the cramped barracks where they were housed. This may have reduced risk of exposure, but it made the workers miserable. The company hauled in staple food, and workers could buy additional items out of a commercial truck at inflated prices. But with nearby ocean beaches off-limits, there was no opportunity for real leisure. Trips to the laundromat were prohibited, and workers faced the futile task of washing their mud-caked clothes by hand. An employee told the *New York Times* that working for Lipman under those conditions, "you're practically a slave." The company was able to enforce the confinement because workers all depended on it not only for their wages and housing but also for the H2-A temporary visas that allowed them to work in the United States legally.[31]

Greenhouse warming and the pandemic converged on California's produce farms as much of the state was engulfed in a record-shattering outbreak of wildfires. Smoke inhalation caused widespread respiratory problems, aggravating Covid-19 symptoms in workers already infected and making previously healthy workers more vulnerable to infection. Many carried on in the fields, because they could not survive without the meager wages.

Exploitation of farmworkers in the name of increased production did nothing to address the worsening plight of the nation's hungry. With tens of millions suddenly out of work in 2020, food pantries and SNAP (the federal "food stamp" program) were deluged with new clients and applicants, many of them seeking food aid for the first time in their lives. Just before the pandemic hit, there were 1.1 million children living in households without enough food to eat during the preceding week. By early 2021, there were 7 to 11 million such children. The growing numbers of the hungry included 28 percent of all children living in Black and Latino households, in contrast to 10 percent of children in white households.[32] Many such families lived in what the Agriculture Department calls "food deserts," places offering inadequate access to healthy and affordable foods. That's the polite name. Leah Penniman says she stays away from the term "food desert," because "it implies a natural phenomenon. It implies a beautiful ecosystem that arose through a natural process. When in fact, there's nothing natural at all about certain people relegated to food opulence and others to food scarcity, often on the lines of race. That's really apartheid."[33]

HUMAN HEALTH VERSUS NATURE'S HEALTH?

WE LEARNED IN 2020 that the interaction between a public health crisis, a climate emergency, systemic racism, and exploitation of workers is complicated. For example, many of the necessary safety precautions developed to reduce exposure to Covid-19 were involved use of the climate-unfriendly personal vehicle: avoidance of public transit, curbside store pickup, drive-through virus testing and vaccination, drive-up food banks and church services, and even parking-lot campaign rallies, where horn-tooting substituted for applause. People living without cars were clearly at a disadvantage when it came to living life in pandemic-time. But vehicle use could also boost viral spread. Research shows that in cities, high population density was not necessarily a cause of high infection rates; rather, the chief factor promoting infection was a high degree of mobility and inter-connectedness with surrounding areas, primarily by road vehicle.[34]

The towering quantities of plastic waste generated by the use of disposable face shields, gowns, gloves, bags, tubes, masks, and other medical equipment created another dramatic ecological problem. Medical wastes are especially troublesome, because they can harbor pathogens and therefore usually must be incinerated. The more such plastic is used and incinerated, the greater the energy use, air pollution, and, potentially, need for adding new incineration capacity. Some nonmedical pandemic-time anomalies, such as increased demand for food delivery or takeout and the increase in disposable packaging used by online vendors for shipping, also produced mountains of extra waste.

The trade publication *The Packer* reported in February 2021, "Now in its second year, the COVID-19 pandemic has given a boost to packaging sales, marketers agree." A major new customer was the U.S. Department of Agriculture's Coronavirus Food Assistance Program, which distributed 132 million "family size" cardboard boxes during 2020. Supermarkets increasingly sold their fresh produce in packaged portions rather than in bulk, to reduce touching of the merchandise. A marketer told *The Packer*, "Consumer sized packaging that fall in the 2- to 5-plus-pound size range is still in high demand. With the stigma of loose vegetables due to COVID, the retailers, along with the consumers, are preferring the more consumer-sized packaging for the fresh produce." Promoting these "grab-and-go" purchases, said another packaging marketer, "elevates food safety, as compared to bulk, loose displays."[35]

The strands connecting Covid-19 with another ecologically problematic technology, air conditioning, are even more tangled. The summer of 2020 had its share of intense heat waves, something that we have come to expect as carbon dioxide accumulates in the atmosphere. Air conditioning helps prevent heat stress during such times, but the greenhouse gas emissions resulting from its continuous, lavish use, not only during local heat waves but for months on end throughout the country, guarantee that future summers will be even hotter. In a further contradiction, air-conditioning makes it easier for people to stay safe at home during a pandemic, but it becomes a threat to public health when larger numbers of people congregate in indoor spaces away from home. The summer heat in 2020 drove meetings, social gatherings, and other group activities into efficiently sealed air-conditioned spaces, where risk of infection in any season can be twenty times as high as outdoors. In a statement published in midsummer by the journal *Clinical Infectious Diseases*, more than 240 scientists warned that in enclosed spaces, airborne, virus-laden "microdroplets" exhaled by an infected person could easily travel the length of a room and be inhaled by another person.

The widely recommended six-foot distancing between people, they wrote, offered little protection in the closed-up indoors. The group urged that occupied indoor spaces be amply ventilated with outdoor air, something that can be accomplished, they wrote, simply by keeping windows open.[36] But open windows aren't compatible with air-conditioning, so their advice was rarely followed. Therefore, the well-known tendency of respiratory viruses to spread more quickly when people gather indoors in the winter months was recapitulated in the Sun Belt during the summer of Covid-19.

Aerosols—the "microdroplets" that the 240 scientists warned about—can accumulate quickly when one or more infected people gather with others in a nicely zipped-up, air-conditioned space. And air-conditioning raises the risk further by lowering the indoor relative humidity. Studies show that coronaviruses in general, including those that cause the common cold, remain viable and infective longer when humidity is low. Furthermore, the water in large or medium exhaled droplets can evaporate very rapidly in an air-conditioned room, producing clouds of much smaller aerosols that can stay aloft in an enclosed space for as long as nine minutes, waiting to be inhaled. Case studies of outbreaks—in an air-conditioned restaurant in China, at a choir practice in a U.S. church, and in numerous bars—provided hints that long-distance drift of infective aerosols could be a hazard in poorly ventilated spaces. Then, in August 2020, scientists captured viable, infective coronavirus from the air of a hospital room almost twenty feet away from the room's one patient.[37]

A conference hosted indoors in Los Angeles in late January 2021 by a high-profile technology executive, Peter Diamandis, provided striking circumstantial evidence that potential airborne transmission by asymptomatic people must be taken seriously. Even though all eighty attendees, panelists, and support staff repeatedly tested negative for the coronavirus before and during the conference, at least twenty, including Diamandis, came down with Covid within a week of the event's end. If family members of the victims are counted, the toll was probably well above thirty people infected. (Given then-current local health orders, the gathering was probably illegal. And in a year of endless ironies, Diamandis's situation stood out. An early Covid denier, he ended up cofounding a Covid vaccine company called Covaxx. Furthermore, his patrons had convened in Los Angeles to discuss some of his reportedly favorite topics, including artificial intelligence, longevity, and exponential growth—the last of which is not only the engine of capitalism and the cause of ecological breakdown but also the mathematical means by which the novel coronavirus brought the U.S. economy to its knees.)[38]

Racial and class disparities in the impacts of climate disruption—this time manifesting as the triple threat of heat, drought, and wildfire—were on frightening display in California in the late summer of 2020. As smoke from the fires thickened, people living in low-income communities already plagued by illnesses associated with poor air quality and the coronavirus found themselves breathing air that was downright dangerous. The smoke from the wildfires was laden with tiny ash particles that when inhaled can cause not only respiratory problems but also strokes and heart attacks. And by 2020 the smoke was also increasing the lungs' susceptibility to the pandemic virus. While affluent Californians were escaping to distant second homes or thousand-dollar-per-night vacation rentals, low-income and unemployed residents were stuck. They could seal up the house and run the air-conditioning—if, that is, they had air-conditioning, could afford the electricity to run it, and were not sweating through a fire-induced power outage. Those who didn't have cooling were compelled to shelter indoors in the intense heat with smoke seeping in, even if they had closed their windows and put rolled-up wet towels at door thresholds.[39] The affluent who didn't flee could run their air conditioning freely (contributing to greenhouse emissions and power blackouts) and buy expensive diesel generators to keep the cool air coming during blackouts, thereby worsening outdoor air pollution even further. They could also afford indoor air purifiers and air-quality sensors. And if things got too bad, they could head for Montana, Hawaii, or other places that were relatively smoke-free and Covid-safe at the time.

When Silicon Valley's air quality deteriorated to "hazardous," lots of millionaires either hightailed it or fortified their high-tech homes against the smoke, leaving low-income residents coughing. Antonio Lopez, a writer and then–City Council candidate in East Palo Alto, told the *Washington Post*, "We talk about the digital divide. Now we're having an air purifier and an AC divide....What gets me is that we're having this conversation in American cities. And not just in American cities but American cities that are in proximity to the most affluent places in the world. It's bizarre, and it's jarring."[40]

THIS IS YOUR WAKE-UP CALL

THE NUMBER ONE reason that a wave of viral infection and death spread through the United States in 2020 was a breakdown of governmental function. In a 2018 afterword to his 2004 book *The Great Influenza*, John Barry writes that during the 1918 flu pandemic that killed at least 675,000 people in the United States and 50 million people worldwide, public officials had sown fear and confusion among the public "not by exaggerating the disease but by trying to reassure." President Woodrow Wilson never mentioned the flu publicly. Other public officials and the media completely dismissed the flu threat, urging that the real danger was panic; almost every newspaper headline about the flu, Barry writes, could have been translated into the same three words: "Don't Get Scared!" But when readers were seeing people falling ill and dying all around them, their reaction to such clearly deceptive reassurances was, naturally, to panic. The situation was exacerbated by doctors touting useless "remedies" that included spraying irritating chemicals into the respiratory system to stimulate mucus flow; drenching the mouth, digestive tract, and skin with alkaline compounds; injecting typhoid vaccines; and administering the malaria treatment quinine. Citing all of the pandemics between 1918 and 2009, Barry wrote that the most serious problem always lay in "the relationship between governments and the truth. Part of that relationship requires political leaders to understand the truth—and to be able to handle the truth."[41] Without knowing it yet, he was also writing about 2020.

Donald Trump's inability to handle the truth, along with his (and his enablers') deep aversion to speaking the truth, supercharged the spread of the coronavirus. (In one of many parallels with 1918, Trump erroneously promoted the malaria drug hydroxychloroquine, a synthetic cousin of 1918's quinine, as a treatment for Covid-19.) Leaders at all levels of government pushed "re-opening" measures that scientists had clearly warned would increase viral spread. But the problem started at the top: Decision after decision and statement after statement emanating directly from the White House or issued through government agencies intentionally blocked government actions that could have suppressed transmission. The result was hundreds of thousands of needless deaths.

Team Trump's response to the coronavirus almost precisely paralleled its response to the climate crisis. Trump's administration denied scientific evidence and attacked scientists or officials who affirmed it; cut agencies' funding and programs; falsified government reports; deleted information from government websites; claimed the issue was a hoax perpetrated by Democrats or foreigners; attacked state and local governments; and, wherever possible, undercut efforts to solve the problem.

Covid-19 disinformation has also fed racism. Throughout 2020 into 2021, verbal and physical assaults against Asian Americans proliferated. One-third of respondents to a national poll said they had personally witnessed the blaming of Asians for the pandemic. The *Washington Post* reported that "New York City's hate crimes task force investigated 27 incidents [against Asians] in 2020, including 24 tied to the coronavirus, a ninefold increase from the previous year." As classrooms began re-opening in 2021, many Asian and Asian American parents continued with online learning for their children, partly out of fear of racist harassment at school. Much of the abuse was fomented by Trump's racist anti-Chinese statements, but Rep. Mark Takano (D-Calif.) cautioned that Trump wasn't the whole story, saying "This sort of bias is latent throughout American society, and it gets worse or less worse depending on the moment."[42] The onslaught turned tragically worse in March 2021 with a shooting rampage at three Atlanta-area massage parlors that left eight people—six of them Asian women—dead. When local law officers apprehended the perpetrator, they seemed eager to convince the public that a 21-year-old white man was definitely not an anti-Asian racist. "During his interview," a local sheriff told reporters, "he gave no indicators that this was racially motivated....We asked him that specifically and the answer was no." A police captain later said of the victim, "He was pretty much fed up and had been kind of at the end of his rope...Yesterday was a really bad day for him." For days, major news media headlined these sham-naïve quotes while tiptoeing around the obvious element of anti-Asian hate.[43] *Daily Show* host Trevor Noah, who grew up in apartheid-era South Africa, highlighted the absurdity of the sheriff's claim by addressing himself to the killer: "Your murders speak louder than your words." He went on to say, "Racism, misogyny, gun violence, mental illness...this incident might have been all of those things combined, because it doesn't have to be one thing on its own. America is a rich tapestry of mass shooting motivations."[44]

Aside from vaccine developers, the private sector performed no better than governments in mitigating the pandemic. Through lobbying and advertising, corporate America was as responsible as Team Trump for undermining efforts to suppress viral spread, all in the interest of profit. Even during the worst outbreaks, TV news programs featuring interviews with public health experts on the urgent need to wear masks and avoid indoor gatherings would then break

for commercials that depicted crowded airports, lively indoor restaurants and dinner parties, and bustling open-plan offices, with no
masks in sight and sometimes featuring the message that the country
was "opening up again." This also had close parallels with climate
messaging—for example, in advertisers' longtime habit of providing news reports on wildfires, heat waves, floods, and other climatic
disasters followed by advertisements for automobiles, airlines, an
abundance of superfluous household goods, and even oil and gas
companies.

From top to bottom, through the entire system, bad decisions
grew out of an impulse to promote business and corporate interests, whatever the jeopardy to fellow human beings or the rest of the
natural world. Millions suffered without pay during closures and
lockdowns, and their plight was used as a pretext to restart businesses unsafely. Getting the economy back on the track of overproduction and overconsumption trumped all other goals, despite the
risk to public health and, inevitably, increased greenhouse emissions. Returning to the pre-Covid "normal"—excess production and
unlimited consumption—remained the priority, despite the fact that
the pre-2020 U.S. economy had delivered as promised only for the
top of the pyramid and had stood in the way of economic justice,
racial justice, and environmental justice. Getting back to normal, the
professed goal of both the political and the medical establishment,
would only mean getting back to overproduction, exploitation,
inequality, and unequal protection under the law.

Many U.S. leaders argued that until the day when vaccines would
swoop in and rescue civilization, we would have no choice but to
plunge into freewheeling economic activity, risking sickness and
death, in the interest of growth. The journalist David Wallace-Wells
pointed to an ironic result: The two nations that outpaced all others in numbers of vaccinations administered during the winter and
spring of 2021—the United Kingdom and the United States—had
also failed to employ effective public health measures and ended up

among the fifteen nations with the world's highest Covid death rates, joined by only two other nations with large economies and populations: Italy and Brazil. Wallace-Wells wrote, "In this sense, the western response to the pandemic is almost a caricature of neoliberalism: indifference to human suffering and unwillingness to disrupt the quotidian churn of a prosperous economy, combined with high-end scientific genius and capital-intensive investment by state actors in profit-oriented innovation, the fruits of which are then hoarded by the global rich (in this case, Americans)."[45] If we allow ourselves to be duped into believing that disaster can only be averted by commercial technologies and not personal and collective practices, then a future rife with climate and human-rights catastrophes is inevitable.

Covid nevertheless helped awaken us to how we overvalue the "normal." In a paper published mid-pandemic in the journal *Organization*, an international group of scholars wrote, "The world is waiting for the pandemic to pass so the economy can grow again and life can resume as normal. But what if normal was the problem in the first place?...Can the pandemic crisis allow us to imagine radical transformations that are not contingent on a model of endless economic growth and that can bring about a more just and regenerative world?" They stressed that "the mechanistic pursuit of economic growth, which is the fundamental basis of the global capitalist political economy, is largely responsible for the current state of the world—a state rife with concentrated wealth but increasingly impoverished in ecological integrity and social wellbeing."[46]

When faced with catastrophe, we, both as individuals and as societies, have a strong tendency to look for all sorts of silver linings. The economy may be hit hard, but, we're told, recovery will grow out of the "creative destruction" wrought by the disaster, churning out jobs and business opportunities and jump-starting even faster growth. Meanwhile, disasters present public officials with opportunities to prove to the public, particularly voters, why the government is important and necessary. In the wake of disaster, local communities also benefit when the need to rescue, recover, and rebuild brings people together in common cause. Pre-disaster hatchets are buried, and mutual aid becomes the order of the day. At least that's what we're told. This last type of silver lining rarely appears in real life—few if any were spotted in 2020—and when it does, the spirit of "we're all in this together" tends to last for a couple of weeks at the most. There's one more post-calamity silver lining, though, that is anticipated more fervently than any other: the wake-up call. We the people and our government, the hope goes, will look at the disaster and its causes and resolve not to repeat past mistakes. Sometimes that happens, and sometimes it doesn't.[47]

The threats and disasters of 2020 should have dialed several wake-up calls. The urgency of reversing the ecological injustice that triggers new disasters had become more obvious than ever. It had become crystal clear that reversing the damage must include the elimination of fossil fuels and their emissions. And there could be no disputing that the causes of marginalization and vulnerability to the multiplying injustices we find ourselves facing—inequality, poverty, housing discrimination, racism, disparities in political power, lack of health care and other public services, and more—must be eliminated.

This all must be done by us all together, not in isolation and not piecemeal. In 1967, in what would be his last Christmas Eve sermon at Atlanta's Ebenezer Baptist Church, Dr. Martin Luther King proclaimed, "It really boils down to this: that all life is interrelated. We are all caught in an inescapable network of mutuality, tied into a single garment of destiny. Whatever affects one directly affects all indirectly. We are made to live together because of the interrelated structure of reality."[48]

The global nature of Covid-19 illustrates King's message that all life is interrelated. The task now is to translate that message into action. Writing in the early months of the pandemic, a group of European researchers discussed how the response to Covid-19 could point societies toward eliminating greenhouse emissions. To paraphrase their conclusions: If behavioral changes like distancing, staying at home, and mask-wearing became routine around the world, then maybe climate-related changes such as using less energy, eating less meat, and traveling less can also become widespread. If capacity can be built to monitor and manage emergency measures such as virus testing and tracing, then monitoring for and ensuring universal energy access, banning utility disconnections and evictions, and preventing overconsumption can be made to stick. If governments can meet the need to finance pandemic response and recovery "in ways commensurate to a grand challenge," they can finance the buildup of green infrastructure, along with social safety nets, income support, universal basic services, and other programs necessary in a low-emissions economy. If we can "restor[e] economic activity gradually and via approaches that are backed by science (e.g., mandatory lockdowns and partial reopening, deployment of government rescue and stimulus funds)," we can also repair the economic damage left by the pandemic in a way that will not overshoot economic limits but will democratize economic power. Similarly, if we can "utiliz[e] a variety of trusted institutions and individuals to convey information and messages" about a pandemic in progress, we can do it in a way that leads to deep, rapid emissions reductions. And if such a full-court press against a pandemic can be accomplished while protecting those more vulnerable to the disease, effective action can also be taken on the climate emergency while ensuring justice and sufficiency for all, including the most vulnerable.[49] But, as we saw in 2020, none of that will happen automatically. Like an alarm clock, a disaster's wake-up call rouses us but doesn't get us out of bed and on the way to work. This requires full-blown mobilization, with diverse leadership giving voice to all sectors of U.S. society.

The fact that some U.S. localities and many countries around the world successfully took action in response to the pandemic may indeed bode well for future climate response. But, alas, the failure of countries such as the United States and Brazil to respond to Covid-19 did not inspire much confidence that the world will at long last take effective climate action. Furthermore, it remains to be seen if any countries build back over the long term in ways that avoid over-shooting ecological limits and maintaining unjust and exploitative relations. The European researchers argue that we face a fork in the road and that "the opportunities emerging from the pandemic for energy systems and climate policy can be secured or squandered. Without careful guidance, governance and consideration, the brave new age wrought by Covid-19 could very well collapse in on itself with bloated stimulus packages, misaligned incentives, the embed-ding of unsustainable practices, and acute and troubling conse-quences for vulnerable groups."

HOPE IN THE STREETS

THE YEAR 2020 also prompted a political/economic discussion the likes of which I had not heard before in my lifetime. It arose when the many lockdown and reopening orders forced elected officials and the public to think about and wrangle over which goods and services are essential and must be provided, and which are nonessential and can be safely suspended. During World War II, the entire U.S. economy came to be shaped by such questions, and equitable access to essen-tials was secured. But in 2020, the debate was largely unenlightening, as when nail salons and tattoo parlors were declared essential dur-ing Georgia's early reopening, or when the White House announced that Vice President Mike Pence would continue traveling and speak-ing at election rallies despite having been exposed to several of his infected staffers, on the grounds that he was an "essential worker." At other times, the "essential" designation effectively sacrificed the health of low-wage workers in order to keep profits rising. People in the United States, for example, could have lived without beef, pork, and poultry for a few months if meat workers had been allowed to

stay home with income support, but that didn't happen. The corporations that control the market would have lost money, and ranchers
would have had no one to sell to. Too many politicians and business owners considered a massive, continent-wide outbreak to be an
acceptable price for keeping the money pipeline flowing. Cruise lines,
clearly nonessential services that had been among the first explosive
infection hot spots, were idled for some time, but some cruises began
returning to the seas and rivers as early as mid-2020. (Later, in the
fall, the first cruise ship to venture back into the Caribbean had to
return to port when a passenger tested positive for Covid-19 on the
first day out.) Some observers noted that cruises should have been
banned decades ago over their exploitation of workers and heavy
impact on the oceans and atmosphere. The pandemic could have
provided an opportunity to abandon them permanently, but securing
profit for owners and investors was prioritized instead.

For a time, despite all the nonsense, 2020 did seem to be teaching
us that we could do things we'd never considered before. Individuals,
households, neighborhoods, cities and towns, and entire states
stepped away from normal life, taking drastic actions (and, crucially,
many necessary *in*actions, such as refraining from air travel) that
would have been deemed wholly unrealistic just weeks earlier. The
fact is, the crises of 2020 demonstrated that people and governments
are capable of suspending business as usual in order to deal with
disaster in real time. The path to a livable future is there—will we
choose to follow it?

The path seemed nearly closed off by the premature business
re-openings, the police riots, the gatherings of guys playing soldier
dress-up and wielding AR-15s, the mask wars, and the checkout-
line fistfights of 2020. But it was kept alive by the uprising against
systemic racism that ignited coast to coast and around the world
through the summer. Maybe, it began to seem, 2020 really could be
a historic turning point, fueling grassroots action on a broad front,
not only against racism and cop violence but also against the many

societal ills, including our assault on the Earth, that both intensify racism and are fed by it.

The expulsion of Trump from the White House—and of his insurrectionist mob from the Capitol—would not end the climate emergency or systemic racism or economic exploitation, and it would not come in time to prevent tens or hundreds of thousands more Covid-19 deaths. But without his defeat, there would have remained little hope that any of the grave crises that converged in 2020 could be resolved before it was too late. Now, would climate, justice, and economic policies deemed outrageously radical before 2020 finally get traction in grassroots America by, say, the midterm elections of 2022? Could it even be possible to end the overproduction and over-consumption that's threatening the Earth, and to do it in a way that ensures sufficiency for communities currently relegated to undercon-sumption of basic needs? Could systemic racism finally be abolished? With Trump gone, there was hope. But time was running out.

2.

THE TANGLED ROOTS OF OUR PREDICAMENTS

Because human activities cause this environmental damage, our species is culpable for a crime we are committing against ourselves. But in our defense, humanity is largely trapped by the political form of liberal state power, which facilitates the smooth functioning of global capitalism—the source of the problem.

—Adrian Parr, 2016[50]

A S THE DREADFUL year 2020 drew to a close, no more than baby steps had yet been taken toward police reform or racial justice. The serious shutdowns that could have brought Covid-19 under control hadn't happened. After an initial relief package expired, the Republican-controlled Senate became exceedingly stingy with economic or social support for either working or unemployed people, insisting instead that people feed their families by staying at or returning to jobs that were either nonexistent or potentially deadly health hazards. And the word "climate" had crossed few lips, masked or unmasked, on Capitol Hill.

Looking back, we can now see why federal and state decision-makers' pandemic response failed. Most of them could not tolerate restricting any part of the economy, because to them, the fundamental goal of society was not the health and well-being of all people but rather economic growth. For the sake of growth, shutdowns were imposed too late and lifted too early. It was regarded as essential that goods be manufactured and services be provided whether they were essential or not; this was capitalism, and rules were rules. Many millions of people were pushed back into risky workplaces in order to keep money flowing, whether or not society needed the products and services being offered. This process was advertised as the only way to keep families fed and housed, but that wasn't true. Adding $600 to weekly unemployment payments had been highly successful through the summer and would have allowed as many people as necessary to remain housed and fed until it was safe to go back to work. When the supplements stopped, poverty and hunger soared. All the "get America back to work" rhetoric was really aimed at keeping business profitable and boosting growth.

Noting that the compulsion for growth lay behind the failure not only of pandemic responses but also of climate policies and even of democracy itself, Julia Steinberger, a professor of social ecology at the University of Lausanne, wrote in 2020, "We are not in democracies where the people can decide their own fate collectively: We are in growth-ocracies where life-saving measures are halted if they impede the accumulation of wealth through profits."[51] The time has come to abandon the old economic system designed to enrich the few and to replace it with one forged by all to benefit all. The path to a livable future must be one with public health, ecological balance, racial justice, and democracy at the center of policy.

LIVING BETWEEN PANDEMICS

THE CLIMATE EMERGENCY'S roots reach deep into humanity's overexploitation of fossilized energy and living ecosystems. It has become apparent as well that the growing threat of pandemics like Covid-19 has its roots in similar soil. With ecological degradation ongoing, new pathogens, most notably viruses, are all but certain to move into the human population from other species. We will likely have no immune defenses against them, and some, like the more dangerous coronavirus variants that have emerged between mid-2020 and the time of this writing in 2021, will have the ability to infect large populations rapidly. We now must prepare to face the increasingly extreme consequences of global warming and outbreaks of deadly new diseases at the same time. We must brace for the possibility that each year to come will find us living either during a pandemic or between pandemics.

The first novel coronavirus thought to have jumped from infected bat populations to humans was SARS-CoV-1. This pathogen caused a pandemic of the deadly disease known as "severe acute respiratory syndrome" (SARS) in 2002–2003. Then, within eighteen short years, we saw two more bat coronaviruses jump to humans: MERS-CoV, which caused an outbreak of Middle East respiratory syndrome (MERS) in 2012, and then in 2019, the SARS-CoV-2 virus, which unleashed the Covid-19 pandemic.

More viruses that originate in other species and cause diseases in humans—what scientists call zoonotic diseases—are probably on the way. Other known bat coronaviruses in the SARS genetic "family" have all the components that made the three recent zoonotic coronaviruses contagious and deadly, and they have been shown to infect and sicken laboratory mice. These and other viruses are likely to be capable of human-to-human transmission, but they are also able to infect other animal species, from which, in turn, they could jump to humans. For example, the MERS virus came to us by way of dromedary camels. All of this suggests that many coronaviruses capable of infecting humans remain at large. "Because we have only just begun to sample, sequence, and study bat/mammalian coronaviruses, we can be certain that what we now know is but the tip of a very large iceberg," wrote ten scientists who represent a broad range of medical disciplines. According to their assessments in 2020, the data "reaffirm what has long been obvious: that future coronavirus transmissions into humans are not only possible, but likely. Scientists knew this years ago and raised appropriate alarm. Our prolonged deafness now exacts a tragic price."[52]

That new pathogens are entering the human population from other animal species at an accelerating pace is no fluke. Human encroachment on landscapes worldwide not only has degraded ecosystems and accelerated greenhouse warming, but it is also increasing the probability of zoonotic diseases and potential pandemics. Invasive corporate agriculture, mining, logging, chemical pollution, and general destruction of biodiversity degrade and destroy wildlife habitats, pushing pathogen-bearing animals to migrate closer to humans. Other eco-disruptive activities can also raise the pandemic threat. Suburban sprawl and tourism (especially "eco-tourism") bring humans closer to wildlife. Hunting involves the most direct contact with wild animals; in fact, it may have been the hunting and capture of live horseshoe bats that led to humans becoming infected with Covid-19. Domestic animal farming, the scale of which far surpasses that of hunting, has produced many more zoonotic infections than any other activity. And we have seen that once a virus or other pathogen gains a foothold in our species, the human propensity for long-distance travel can quickly turn a local outbreak into a pandemic.

In some cases, human-induced greenhouse warming is creating conditions for the spread of zoonotic infection. In East and North Africa, for example, droughts have become more frequent and intense thanks to climate change. Many pastoralists have responded by replacing their cattle herds with camels, which, famously, can survive for long stretches of time without access to water. As a result, much larger numbers of camels are now in close contact with humans in the region. Worryingly, the coronavirus that causes MERS is circulating in camel populations in several countries in the region, putting the lives of their handlers at very high risk. In outbreaks since 2012, one-third of the more than 2,500 people infected with the MERS virus have died from it.[53]

Our encroachment on the ecosphere has opened a Pandora's box. Bat coronaviruses, scientists warn, are "functionally preadapted" to infecting humans. That preadaptation may be related to similarities among bats, minks, cats, humans, and some other mammalian species in our lung-cell membranes' susceptibility to entry by this group of viruses. Three different coronaviruses that cause severe disease in cattle, horses, and swine are closely related to another virus that has long been causing the common cold in humans. These livestock viruses potentially could acquire, through genetic exchange, the ability to infect us.[54]

In a 2020 article in the journal *Cell*, David Morens and Anthony Fauci (the latter an eminent infectious-disease expert who in 2020 became the most widely trusted U.S. authority on Covid) wrote of pathogens that are newly emerging in human populations:

> SARS, MERS, and COVID-19 are only the latest examples of a deadly barrage of coming coronavirus and other emergences. The COVID-19 pandemic is yet another reminder, added to the rapidly growing archive of historical reminders, that in a human-dominated world, in which our human activities represent aggressive, damaging, and unbalanced interactions with nature, we will increasingly provoke new disease emergences. We remain at risk for the foreseeable future. COVID-19 is among the most vivid wake-up calls in over a century. It should force us to begin to think in

earnest and collectively about living in more thoughtful and creative harmony with nature, even as we plan for nature's inevitable, and always unexpected, surprises.[55]

Clearly, many of the activities that can lead to emergence of zoonotic diseases—deforestation, mining, roadbuilding, sprawl, intrusion into wilderness, travel and tourism, factory farming of animals and crops—also produce greenhouse-gas emissions and other pollution. Likewise, some of the more prominent threats to the ecosphere—travel by ground, air, or sea; air-conditioning—also accelerate person-to-person spread of coronaviruses and other pathogens. With the roots of climate and public health emergencies intermingling in the abuse of landscapes and resources, civilization's survival now depends on reversing ecological degradation worldwide.

LIVING BETWEEN HEAT WAVES

IT WAS STILL possible—even in 2020—to create doubt about what should have been an obvious causal link between greenhouse warming and, say, the wildfires then scouring much of the West Coast and Rockies or the supercharged hurricanes that were slamming into the Gulf Coast. Part of the problem was that most liberal politicians and activists were talking more and more about climate policy as if it should be no more than a vehicle for delivering good jobs and cleaner technology. Not enough was said about the direct peril we increasingly face by failing to eradicate fossil fuel use quickly enough. The immediate ravages of the pandemic were making clear the need to wear masks and avoid crowds; in contrast, despite the wildfires and hurricanes, people were not clearly seeing the disaster that loomed in their future and the future of generations to come. It's not that the grimness of that future was a deep secret. Back in 2008, Mark Lynas's book *Six Degrees* had painted a scary picture of a world warming degree by degree toward non-survivability, and he had published an updated version in 2020. The Intergovernmental Panel on Climate Change projected some catastrophic results of even a two-degree rise, in its 2018 report *Global Warming of 1.5° C.*[56] But the hair-raising details of what could lie ahead for this and future generations are still not getting through to most people in the United States.

Discussions of the greenhouse future tend to focus on fires, storms, and rising seas, and that orientation has fostered a belief that for affluent countries, armoring against and adapting to those problems can be factored in as a cost of doing business. A 2020 *ProPublica* article titled "Climate Change Will Force a New American Migration" demolished that expectation. In it, the reporter Abrahm Lustgarten used the projections of climate models to paint a picture of a torrid future, one that we could never buy our way out of. He argued that if we fail to taken radical action against greenhouse emissions and instead allow a constant, relentless ratcheting up of temperatures, the lives of North Americans will be permanently upended. In coastal, rural, and southern regions, he wrote, many communities could find themselves at "the brink of collapse" in coming decades. "This process has already begun in rural Louisiana and coastal Georgia," writes Lustgarten, "where low-income and Black and Indigenous communities face environmental change on top of poor health and extreme poverty." Those who can afford to leave will head north; those who cannot will find themselves faced with increasingly adverse conditions. In summer, the entire Mississippi Valley will be gripped by heat and humidity so oppressive that the country will be bisected by a vast stretch of territory that will be practically uninhabitable for much of the year. At the same time, extreme water shortages will occur periodically across the entire country west of Missouri. Thanks to the growing threat of fire and smoke, one out of ten San Francisco Bay area residents will be forced to migrate out—in Marin County, it could rise to one in four. Heat and drought could trigger "megafires" not only in the West, but even in Texas, Florida, and Georgia. Rural areas of the Sun Belt will depopulate, with millions crowding into the region's already stressed big cities.

It's already happening in Georgia. According to Lustgarten, "Atlanta—where poor transportation and water systems contributed to the state's C+ infrastructure grade last year—already suffers greater income inequality than any other large American city, making it a virtual tinderbox for social conflict. One in 10 households earns less than $10,000 a year, and rings of extreme poverty are growing on its outskirts even as the city center grows wealthier."[57] The Sun Belt's more affluent residents will flee north. Duluth, Buffalo, and other small to medium-size cities on the Great Lakes, with their relatively cool summers and ample water supplies, are already being eyed as climate refuges. Millions living in the southern half of the country are expected to move to northern metropolitan areas, leading to "chaotic urbanization," breakdowns of public services, and increased poverty rates.

With the continuation of business as usual, global sea level will rise several more feet, permanently transforming eight of the twenty most populous U.S. cities. As a result, an estimated 50 million people will be forced to somehow adapt or move away. Miami will be first. Within a few decades, Miami-Dade County will become a chain of small islands, in a sense taking the place of the Florida Keys; today's Keys will be completely submerged. Most of Miami-Dade County's inhabitants, currently numbering 2.7 million, will depart. The Miami archipelago will end up a community full of second homes belonging to rich investors or retirees who have summer homes up North.

Already, Miami is seeing a pernicious trend of "climate gentrification." A prime target is the low-income Little Haiti neighborhood, which lies on what passes for high ground in Miami: seven to ten feet above sea level. As Miami Beach, Brickell, and other low-lying upscale neighborhoods see more frequent bouts of coastal flooding, properties will decline in value, so developers are already prowling Little Haiti and other high spots, buying up lots. An exodus of the neighborhood's predominantly Black population is already beginning.[58]

Only radical action to eliminate greenhouse emissions can prevent this widespread internal displacement of climate-stressed populations. We are already seeing such impacts throughout the Americas. People arriving at the U.S. southern border from Central America in recent years have been seeking refuge not only from crime and violence but also from greenhouse-induced drought and crop failures. The U.S. response has ranged from treating refugees as an unfortunate nuisance to practicing extreme cruelty against them. As climate disruption worsens, the numbers of refugees from tropical regions fleeing flood and drought will multiply. Without a strong national movement to counter it, U.S. anti-immigration policy will likely harden and further militarize in response, hastening our drift toward authoritarianism. Jeremy Deaton writes for *Fast Company*:

> Researchers have made some effort to predict how humans will respond to climate change. Studies find that, as the planet warms, people will become less productive and more violent. Rising seas will drive mass migration, and worsening droughts will lead to crop failures, economic downturns, and armed conflicts. Some research even finds that climate change will lead to more nationalism and authoritarianism. But none of these studies can say what, precisely, any of this means for the future of U.S. democracy....Humans are capricious. Our democracy is fragile. Climate change will do more than alter the weather.[59]

The need for strong action is deepened further when we consider the even more dramatic and tragic prospect of the global humanitarian catastrophe that will result if waves of people are forced to migrate out of all of the hot regions that encircle the Earth. People live scattered across the planet's surface, but throughout history, human populations have lived mostly in regions where the air temperature, averaged day and night over 365 days per year, lies within a very narrow range. Not surprisingly, the crops and livestock domesticated by humans over the past 10 thousand years are adapted to those same temperatures. The geographic zones where those civilization-friendly temperatures prevail, as well as our adaptation to the temperatures in those regions, have been remarkably stable for millennia. However, forecasts say that if greenhouse emissions aren't reduced deeply and quickly, those zones are going to shift across the Earth's surface more dramatically in the next fifty years than they have in the past 6 *thousand*. The biggest shifts toward a human-hostile environment will be felt across tropical South America and Africa, the Middle East, South and Southeast Asia, much of China, and the U.S. Sun Belt. Hospitable zones will shift toward the northern United States and southern Canada, Europe (except Spain, Italy, and Greece), Russia, Central Asia, Korea, Japan, and far northern China. Billions of people will be compelled to migrate thousands of miles in order to live in a habitable environment. The impacts on food production will be incalculable.[60]

WHAT WE ALL NEED, AND WHO'S NOT GETTING IT

ECOLOGICAL CATASTROPHE CAN be prevented only through massive climate mobilization, not the continued pursuit of economic growth that only enriches the few. Much research shows that in low-income nations, the provision of essential goods and services improves with a rising Gross Domestic Product (GDP), but only up to a point. Any growth of GDP beyond that required to fully meet those needs does not improve well-being further. At some point in the past, growth in the economies of affluent nations ceased improving their population's well-being but continued to increase energy and material consumption as well as production of greenhouse gases and other pollutants. And thanks to inequality, systemic racism, and other scourges, some nations with bloated, overgrown economies, best exemplified by the United States, are still failing to meet the basic needs of millions of people within their borders. The reason is that free-market mechanisms are incapable of delivering universal well-being; in fact, for marginalized people and communities, the market reliably delivers the opposite: inadequate, unsafe housing, poor or no medical care, hunger, unbreathable air, undrinkable water, electric and water cutoffs, toxic chemicals, vulnerability to disasters, and landscapes devoid of vegetation. For their part, the national, state, and local governments often throw in police violence, mass incarceration, and erosion of social services.

What are the core requirements for an adequate quality of life? Narasimha Rao and Jihoon Min of the International Institute for Applied Systems Analysis in Austria took a shot at answering that question in a 2018 study by developing global "decent living standards," which they defined as material prerequisites for human well-being. They outlined highly specific material elements of a decent life: adequate nutrition, including sufficient daily intake of calories, protein, iron, zinc, and vitamins, as well as a "modest sized" refrigerator; a solidly built home with minimum floor space of at least 315 square feet plus 100 additional square feet per occupant beyond three; electric lighting and "modern" heating and/or cooling equipment, if necessary; a safe, reliable water supply of at least twelve gallons per person per day; good indoor toilets; a "backbone infrastructure" to deliver electricity, water, and sanitation; sufficient clothing appropriate to the local climate as well as a minimum number of shared washing machines per thousand people; and the material requirements for freedom to publicly and peaceably assemble, which they estimated in terms of "minimum public space per thousand inhabitants (with adequate facilities to ensure safety, such as lighting at night)." Rao and Min wrote that globally, "household air pollution (typically from burning biomass) is the third highest health risk factor, leading to over 4 million premature deaths per year, who are mainly women and children." Therefore, decent living standards must include a cooking stove and a heating source that does not pollute indoor air.[61]

Shockingly, many people in the United States do not have access even to Rao and Min's proposed global minimum requirements for a decent standard of living; furthermore, many of those same people and communities are forced to live with the environmental consequences of the overproduction and overconsumption that dominate the economy at large. People lack access to basic necessities in this country and throughout the globe not because the world economy is underproducing goods but because it is producing enormous disparities in consumption among and within countries.

It doesn't have to be this way. In late 2020, Rao, Julia Steinberger, and co-authors showed that it would be physically possible for Earth's human population in 2050 to enjoy universal decent living standards even if total worldwide energy consumption declines to only a little more than half what it is today, assuming rough global equality of access to energy. Unlike current high and rising global energy consumption, the low, equitable, stable energy demand on their Earth of 2050, they estimated, could be supplied entirely from non-fossil, non-nuclear sources.[62]

In the United States, total power generation is sufficient to deliver plenty of electricity to every household. The problem for many households is not availability but cost; many are forced to choose between paying their rent or mortgage and paying their electric or gas bill. Approximately 15 percent of households miss one or more monthly payments for utilities or housing (or both) every year, and they pay a high price in large penalty fees and shutoffs, which only exacerbate the problem.[63] A wholesale transition from power plants fired by coal and gas to wind farms and solar parks would deeply reduce the cost of electricity, and a parallel transition toward electric cooking and space heating, and solar water heating could eliminate gas bills entirely. That transition will take a long time, so some households are jumping ahead with solar power for their own homes. Homeowners who can afford to install rooftop solar enjoy permanently lower energy expenditures than do lower-income home-owners or renters who can't pay the large up-front costs of a rooftop solar array, batteries, inverters, and other equipment. An obvious way to ensure sufficient power to low-income homes while also free-ing them of high utility bills would be to provide or heavily subsidize home solar-power systems for houses, apartment buildings, or entire neighborhoods. Such programs are rare today.

Homegrown energy generation is expanding, but is also plagued by racial and ethnic disparities. A 2019 study by Researchers at Tufts University and the University of California at Berkeley published results in 2019 showing that majority-Black neighborhoods had a 69 percent lower installation rate of rooftop solar than did neighbor-hoods in which no ethnic group was in the majority. Latino-majority neighborhoods had a 30 percent lower rate, while white-majority neighborhoods had 21 percent more rooftop solar. These dispari-ties can be accounted for partly, but not entirely, by differences in income, wealth, and home ownership. In 2016, 58 percent of Black and 54 percent of Latino U.S. residents were renters, whereas the rate for white residents was just 28 percent. And landlords are naturally reluctant to bear the cost of buying and installing rooftop solar when it is the tenants who would enjoy the lower power bills.[64] Melanie Santiago-Mosier, senior director of Vote Solar's Access & Equity Program, responded to the Tufts–UC Berkeley study: "For me, it was like a bucket of ice water in my face that really, really hit home... that despite income and despite homeownership, there's a very pro-nounced disparity in terms of rooftop solar deployment based on race, and that was horrifying for me to read."[65]

The discrepancies in solar use are not for lack of interest. Black and Latino homeowners install rooftop solar at a *higher rate* than white households of comparable income if there is already at least one solar installation in their neighborhood or if they have some contact with the solar-energy industry. Within the industry, however, the white population holds a dominant advantage, accounting for most of the employment overall. The biggest discrepancy is in management and executive positions, 80 percent of which are occupied by white, non-Latino people.[66]

TECHNOLOGY AND THE PERVERSION OF AGRICULTURE

WHITE WESTERN CULTURE'S near-total lack of humility with respect to the living Earth caught up with us in 2020. We paid a high price for our hubris and seem to have learned nothing from the experience. Leaders in the Global North remain wedded to a worldview that Wes Jackson has labeled "technological fundamentalism": the belief that the human economy can rely purely on technical innovation to expand material abundance while easily tidying up the wreckage we inflict on the biosphere in the process.[67] In particular, writes Leah Penniman, the dominant culture fails to acknowledge "the myriad Afro-Indigenous practices" carried out by "those who persist in believing that the land and waters are family members, cling to our ancestral ways of knowing, and continue to practice Earth-based technologies." She urges us all to take that path:

> In this time, we are acutely aware of the fractures in our
> system of runaway consumption and corporate insatiabil-
> ity. We feel the hot winds of wildfire, the disruptions of
> pandemic, and the choked breath of the victims of state
> violence. We know there is no going back to "normal." The
> path forward demands that we take our rightful places as
> the younger siblings in creation, deferring to the oceans, for-
> ests, and mountains as our teachers. Those whose skin is the

color of soil are reviving their ancestral and ancient practice of listening to the Earth to know which way to go. It is by listening that we can heal our society's sickness.[68]

Faced with a raging pandemic, too many political leaders have ignored nature, insisting that waiting for Big Pharma to develop drugs and vaccines (with, in Trump's world, the addition of quack cures and household disinfectants) is the only way to prevent deaths; as a result, tried-and-true human behavioral changes that acknowledge our vulnerability to new zoonotic diseases and could have curbed the pandemic were not pursued effectively. We continue to expand our energy-generating and energy-consuming technologies in false confidence that there will be no backlash from the Earth. Meanwhile, Trump and some local officials launched high-tech military-style assaults on nonviolent Black Lives Matter protests, thereby escalating the situation, when low-tech, respectful discussion was clearly in order.

Consistent with this pattern, the Covid-19 outbreaks that hit farmworkers and food workers especially hard resulted from the technological juicing of agriculture. Fruits and vegetables occupy only about 3 percent of the nation's farmland. Some of that land is in family-owned truck farms, community gardens, and other small-scale production, but much of it is in large operations that depend on industrial technology and vast numbers of mostly migrant workers for harvesting, packing, and processing the produce. Farming on a large industrial scale has had profound side effects for both people and the land. The agriculture and food industry, whose pace and production were once dictated by seasons and weather, has maintained and increased its profits by maximizing output per worker, whether that worker is a Kansas farmer driving a massive wheat combine or an immigrant laborer picking strawberries or cutting up chicken. The speedup's consequences for farmworkers had long been severe; then, during the pandemic, special concessions made to businesses designated as essential allowed the farm and food companies to continue and further tighten the exploitation, endangering the health and lives of workers and their families.

The 2020 treatment of this essential workforce was in keeping with what the economist Michael Perelman labeled the "farm worker paradox" in which he asked why "those whose work is most necessary typically earn the least" (and, considering workers' heavy exposure to toxic chemicals, and especially since the advent of Covid-19, we might add, "and are most strongly compelled to risk their lives and their families' lives"). The paradox exists, observes Perelman, because of the circular logic of capitalism. Economists argue that farmworkers earn low wages because they are not highly "productive"; that is, collectively, they generate low profit per worker. But the industry's profit margins are low because everyday food sells cheap, and it's cheap largely because many of those who produce it must subsist on near-starvation wages.[69]

Although the soft and perishable nature of fresh produce requires that lots of manual labor be employed in its production, harvesting, and handling, those processes have been industrialized in many ways. Mechanization has penetrated even deeper on the much greater acreage, mostly in sparsely populated regions, where staple foods such as wheat, oats, rice, and dry beans are produced. Tractors and farm implements have grown to gargantuan scale in order to allow a single farmer or family to till, fertilize, sow, spray chemicals, harvest, and repeat the sequence on thousands of acres. This factory farming of field crops has led to increased consumption of fossil fuel, for traction and production of fertilizer, chemicals, and machinery. On a worldwide average, three to six kilocalories of mostly fossil energy are consumed in producing, processing, and delivering a single kilocalorie of food energy. For farming in the United States, the ratio is even higher.[70] One result is a large and growing output of greenhouse gas emissions.

Annual tillage has not only caused soil erosion but also destroyed the soil's organic matter, sending even more carbon dioxide into the atmosphere. Rivers in farm country are so polluted by nitrates and pesticides that it is not safe to eat fish from them. Biodiversity, above and below ground, is crashing. In a 2021 article pointedly titled "Underestimating the Challenges of Avoiding a Ghastly Future," seventeen eminent ecologists warned that "since the start of agriculture around 11,000 years ago, the biomass of terrestrial vegetation has been halved," with more than 20 percent of the original biodiversity species lost. Just in the past five hundred years, approximately six hundred plant species and more than seven hundred vertebrate species have gone extinct.[71]

Infection rates remained low during the first few months of the Covid-19 pandemic among the mostly white and independent farming families who produce staple crops and feed grains, scattered as they were across thinly populated regions. Their isolation was enhanced by decades of decline in the number of family farms and the consolidation of land into fewer and fewer hands. But the people of rural America—where migration out of the countryside and small towns has meant a withering of local economies, culture, and health care, as well as an aging of the population—were highly vulnerable to the coronavirus when, inevitably, it came for them. The virus eventually brought extensive suffering and mortality to those rural regions.

There's a parallel to the fruit, vegetable, and staple foods story in U.S. beef, pork, and poultry production. There are the highly industrialized yet labor-intensive processing facilities, staffed with mostly Latino, Black, and Asian, largely immigrant workers who are subject to super-exploitation and disease outbreaks. And scattered across rural America are the places where the animals that supply the industry are raised—confined animal feeding operations—crammed with cattle, swine, and poultry. The negative ecological impacts of factory farming are well documented. Among them are emissions of carbon dioxide, methane, nitrous oxide, and other greenhouse gases. Large volumes of emissions are generated by burning of fossil fuels during the construction and operation of the facilities, in the fields where feed grains are grown and harvested, in fertilizer factories, and in hauling the grain to the facilities. Additional greenhouse gases are released by the animals' metabolic processes, especially in the case of beef cattle. What Henning Steinfeld, Chief of the UN Food and Agriculture Organization's livestock branch, said in 2006 remains true: "Livestock are one of the most significant contributors to today's most serious environmental problems. Urgent action is required to remedy the situation."[72] Vastly downsizing the corporate beef business would free us from a significant source of climate destabilization.

Feedlots and confinement operations are also notorious for producing dangerous quantities of local air and water pollution. Production of corn, soybeans, and other feed grains robs soils of essential plant nutrients—nitrogen, phosphorus, and others—which then end up as pollutants, either in groundwater or streams, or in scrap animal parts at the meat plant. Is factory-farmed meat really an essential industry? Whether it's meat, vegetables, or grains, the dominant U.S. food production systems are hazards both to human health and well-being and to the ecosphere.

AMERICA'S ENERGY CONSUMPTION: BOTH EXCESSIVE AND INSUFFICIENT

IN THE EARLY months of the Covid pandemic, with U.S. economic activity in freefall and, in response, the haze of pollution lifting temporarily from cities, Republican politicians and campaign operatives hit on a new strategy. They would convince voters that those blue skies could mean only one thing: If elected, a Democratic administration and Congress would enact climate proposals like the Green New Deal, which would ruin the economy. With their comically bad cause-and-effect logic, they were glossing over the fact that the very core of the Green New Deal and other Democratic climate plans was economic stimulus, primarily through investment in industrial development. That had been true even before 2020, when the economy was booming and needed only greater equality, not a growth stimulant. More positively, the plans called for the kinds of protections for working and unemployed people that, had they been in place at the start of 2020, would have prevented much of the economic hardship that came as a side effect of the pandemic response. Climate action plans and Democratic post-pandemic recovery plans both have emphasized not only worker protections and economic justice but also racial justice, Indigenous rights, workers' rights, immigrants' rights, social safety nets, and other remedies that would help steer the nation's economy away from the increasingly exploitative, racist path it has taken in recent years. But none of the mainstream climate plans were adequate to end America's contribution to greenhouse warming. They all lacked a necessary element: a direct mechanism to rapidly reduce the use of fossil fuels in the economy, entirely eliminating them on a crash deadline.

The fact that the Republicans voted unanimously against the 2021 American Rescue Plan, which provided for income supports and safety nets in response to the pandemic, further belied claims that their opposition to climate action was motivated by their belief that it would "kill jobs" and hurt ordinary people in the United States. They opposed climate action because they feared it would hurt profits, growth, and the stock market. Whether the proposed climate policies of 2020 would do that is debatable. But if in the future, the one necessary goal that was lacking from all existing climate plans—the direct elimination of fossil fuels—were to become law, it would almost certainly curtail or reverse growth, making those worker supports and safeguards that the Republicans so despised even more important than they already are.

No surefire plan exists for achieving a sweeping conversion that holds the Earth's warming to 1.5 degrees while sustaining growth. The International Energy Agency admitted as much in its 2021 report "Net Zero by 2050: A Roadmap for the Global Energy Sector."[73] The agency—one that no one would ever accuse of being a radical green outfit—concluded that envisioning a path to net-zero global emissions by 2050, while ensuring strong economic growth along the way, requires extraordinary technological leaps of faith. Not only will energy efficiency have to increase at a highly unlikely pace equal to three times the current rate of efficiency improvement. The agency's roadmap further requires that by 2050 almost half of all emissions reductions will come from technologies that are not only unproven—*they have not even been developed yet*. Any projection of economic growth during the energy transition is unrealistic.

In my book *The Green New Deal and Beyond* I cite extensive research and analysis also demonstrating that renewable energy sources can never be scaled up to satisfy 100 percent of current U.S. or world energy demand, let alone growth of that demand. One scenario purporting to achieve that goal would result in wind farms covering 6 percent of the entire land surface of the forty-eight contiguous states. Plans for "100 percent renewable" energy worldwide would require solar installation on at least as many square miles of the Earth's surface as are now occupied by all food production and human settlement combined.[74] Even if such extreme courses of action were possible, they would be ecologically unacceptable.

We will have to live with a more modest energy supply, but even then, renewable power generation will occupy a lot of territory. Transitioning to renewable sources will mean leaving behind a world in which energy is supplied from oil and gas fields, strip mines, power plants, refineries—plots of land that, while socially and ecologically destructive, collectively cover a tiny area compared with the area occupied by all human activities. To replicate current high-energy economies by relying on much more diffuse energy sources such as wind and sunlight would mean harvesting that energy from a total land area vastly larger than that on which we live and work. In that respect, harvesting of wind and solar energy would, in its scale, come to resemble the harvesting of food, lumber, and biomass, all of which are done across vast swaths of the Earth. A long history shows that our far-flung pursuit of natural resources has often had dire consequences for the occupied ecosystems and the Indigenous peoples who lived in harmony with them for many generations without causing harm. Likewise, covering vast land areas with industrial energy installations cannot be done without ecological and humanitarian consequences. They must be placed only where they cause the least ecological harm and do not violate the rights of those living in the region.

A renewable energy buildup will also be dependent on fossil fuels. We will not find a means by which renewable energy can pull itself up by its bootstraps while at the same time filling the growing gap being left by the departure of fossil fuels. In the coming decades, the components, manufacture, delivery, installation, lifetime maintenance, and retirement of renewable energy capacity will be powered by fossil fuels. And in their operation, solar parks and wind farms will be feeding power into an existing grid that will not yet be able to function without the input from fossil-fueled power plants. This is not an argument for the necessity for fossil fuels, but rather a reminder that ridding ourselves of them will not be easy or immediate.

Around the world, electricity makes up 20 to 40 percent of societies' energy consumption. Renewable sources of electricity will be expected not only to displace fossil fuels as the source of the electricity for today's uses, such as lighting, appliances, air-conditioning, the digital world, welding, urban mass transit, and myriad others. Renewables will also have to supply electricity, directly or indirectly, to perform all of the functions that now depend on oil and natural gas, primarily in agriculture, transportation, manufacturing, cooking, and heating, but in many other ways as well—including, eventually, producing and installing new wind and solar installations when current ones wear out. There is no master plan for doing any of that. A group of Australian researchers summed up the situation in 2020 in the journal *Futures*:

> For the foreseeable future the deployment of RE [renewable energy] infrastructure will remain locked via innumerable path dependencies to fossil-fueled industrial production and distribution systems. It is theoretically conceivable that in the future all the processes involved in RE supply system production—including mining, manufacture, and transport—can be powered by renewably generated electricity. But this is subject to a wide range of engineering, economic, and institutional challenges. It will not be possible to anticipate many of the consequences of confronting these. This is no argument against as rapid a deployment of RE technology as humanity can mobilize. Instead, it is a further argument for anticipating societies that require as little energy as possible to flourish, rather than assuming that energy-intensive societies can simply transition to RE technologies without difficulty or disruption.[75]

Building "societies that require as little energy as possible to flourish" would provide the bonus benefit of reducing our negative impact on the Earth and on the living conditions of our fellow humans. In a pandemic-time interview, Robin Wall Kimmerer, a member of the Citizen Potawatomi Nation and author of the book *Braiding Sweetgrass: Indigenous Wisdom, Scientific Knowledge, and the Teachings of Plants*, described a worldview that is far less dependent than today's society on high energy input: "I live in upstate

New York with four very distinct seasons, and it's like having four different lives, and you don't try to control that; you become part of the flow and let it teach you. We just say, 'Now is a chance to celebrate something else, to be part of something else in the cycle.' Being permeable to place and ecology can lead to taking advantage of abundance during times of plenty and then not asking for more. Being content with what has been given, finding sufficiency."[76]

Illustrating the physical fact that when we use industrial energy to perform work, it inevitably alters materials and changes the environment, researcher John Schramski and colleagues write, "Metaphorically, it is not only the origin, quantity, or quality of the gas in your tank, it is what you are doing to the environment with your truck. Thus, for example, it only partially matters if this [energy] is from renewable or non-renewable fuels. We are detonating a large amount of energy in a closed system and causing dramatic environmental change." They conclude that "science has failed to properly convey the extent of runaway energy discharge, its front-seat role in innovation, and its fundamental and dangerous role in the rearrangement of nature."[77]

GROWTH VERSUS WELL-BEING

OPPORTUNITIES AROSE TO create a less gluttonous society during and after the pandemic, but climate leaders and policymakers have rarely called for that. They have focused, and rightly so, on justice and equality but also, excessively, on energy technologies that they believe will eventually replace fossil fuels. Granted, they have talked about cutting subsidies to the fossil fuel companies and disinvesting from them. They've discussed carbon taxes, but it's too late for taxes to work, and that idea is fading. They have called for an end to drilling on public lands, bans on fracking, and prohibition of exports—all excellent ideas. Few, however, have advocated for the one policy that can guarantee that emissions are eliminated: a direct, mandatory mechanism to drive the extraction and burning of oil, gas, and coal down to zero.

Such actions are widely viewed, correctly, as a threat to an unjust economic system centered on endless growth. Limitless growth is neither natural nor sustainable. The Gullah/Geechee community, descendants of enslaved peoples, have been living in a steady-state relationship with nature on the sea islands of South Carolina and Georgia since the 1600s. Queen Quet, chief of the Gullah/Geechee nation, told *The Root* in 2019, "We have never overfished. We do not do building patterns that build into the coastline. We are not people who go out and derby fish, meaning to try and take everything you can out of the creek. We are communal people. One of the critical things is just trying to encourage our younger people to get with the elders so that they know how to live in the traditional way that we live, because that will sustain them. It has been sustaining us and our ancestors for over 400 years."[78]

Ideas for a climate-friendly economic recovery from Covid-19 have been aimed at generic Keynesian growth stimulus. President Biden and Vice President Harris won the 2020 election partly on the strength of their policy proposals for trillions of federal dollars to be invested in a new workforce to build up renewable energy capacity and green infrastructure. A transatlantic survey of more than two hundred central bank and treasury officials in the G20 group of large countries examined various post-pandemic stimulus strategies and concluded, "Recovery packages that seek synergies between climate and economic goals have better prospects for increasing national wealth, enhancing productive human, social, physical, intangible, and natural capital."[79]

Absent from such plans were any provisions for monitoring which sectors of society will be enriched by the wealth to be generated, or the ecological consequences of the growth that is stimulated. Growth is advertised as the only means of creating jobs for all, but in reality, it serves to perpetuate economic and social injustices such as severe distortions in income and wealth distribution. It's a way for the owning and investing classes to maintain and grow the huge share of the national treasure that they hold while leaving behind a little something to keep the nation's working majority functioning. For the rich to keep increasing their percentage of the pie without rendering families of modest income homeless and starving, the pie has to keep getting bigger.

When the pie shrinks, as it did in 2008 and 2020, it's the small slices that are cut even thinner. When the pie is growing, as it did from 2009 through 2019, the big pieces grow first and fastest. At the time the pandemic struck, the incomes of households ranking in the top 33 percent of the income scale, on average, had grown considerably larger than they had been before 2008. But households in the bottom two-thirds were, on average, still struggling to get back to their income levels of twelve years earlier. Then, within a matter of months in 2020, those lower two-thirds saw their hard-won gains evaporate. Not surprisingly, there were racial and ethnic disparities. In New York City, 43 percent of white, 55 percent of Black, and 59 percent of Latino workers suffered loss of income during the course of the pandemic. Rates of food hardship were even more lopsided: 17, 50, and 57 percent, respectively.[80] Over approximately the same period, the 644 wealthiest people in the United States gained almost a trillion dollars in net worth. Some of them more than doubled their wealth, and Amazon boss Jeff Bezos, the world's richest person, saw his wealth rise by almost 80 percent, thanks to a surge in online buying during the pandemic. The total wealth held by U.S. billionaires rose to almost double that of the least wealthy 50 percent of the entire U.S. population.[81] Harvard's Cornel West told the *Guardian* that it was the virus of capitalism—not Covid—that created these disparities: "The virus encounters deeply racist structures and institutions already in place, against the backdrop of wealth inequality, a militarized state, and a commodified culture in which everybody and everything is for sale."[82]

If, in the post-pandemic years, as after 2008, the government aims to rely upon aggregate GDP growth—a bigger pie instead of a re-sliced pie—to restore jobs and incomes, we'll get neither economic sufficiency for all, nor racial justice, nor sustainability. We will see yet another lost decade, with continuing economic hardship for the majority, worsening ecological degradation, increasing output of greenhouse emissions, and more massive wealth for the few.

There's another way in which continued growth in monetary wealth will sustain high greenhouse emissions and resource exploitation, as well as injustice. The largest gains from growth always go to households with already high incomes, and the high purchasing power of the affluent leads inexorably to higher consumption and greenhouse emissions, while also providing them extra measures of protection in the face of public health emergencies like Covid-19. Vehicle ownership, spacious, low-density living spaces, abundant internet access, high-quality health care, safe access to ample food and other necessities, and other privileges all contributed to the yawning gap between rich and poor, and between white and not, in infection and death rates from the coronavirus. The affluent also engage in by far the most air travel, which fueled the early spread of the virus. Then, as the threat to their health grew, they were also easily able to forgo the luxury of flying and log onto Zoom.

The rich build what Naomi Klein has called "their privatized kind of rescue bubbles" to protect them from any disaster. When confronted with disasters like the February 2021, record-breaking freeze and power-grid collapse in Texas, says Klein, the rich and powerful "don't see themselves as part of the public infrastructure that they're systematically allowing to degrade. They believe they'll be fine. What does that look like? It looks like Ted Cruz flying off to Mexico"—infamously, to escape the 2021 Texas power outage. "Now, he got caught. He's calling it a mistake. It's actually a metaphor for the fact that they don't believe they have to deal with the effects of the disasters that they themselves are creating."[83]

In a 2020 paper titled "Scientists' Warning on Affluence," Thomas Wiedmann of the University of New South Wales and his co-authors wrote, "We find that, to a large extent, the affluent life-styles of the world's rich determine and drive global environmental and social impact. Moreover, international trade mechanisms allow the rich world to displace its impact to the global poor." In affluent capitalist economies, relentless pressure to overconsume is exerted even on those with modest incomes. Competition in the labor market drives wage workers toward investment in cars for commuting (and increasingly as a requirement of the job itself, especially in the "gig economy"), communication devices and subscriptions to costly digital services, extra clothing, home labor-saving technologies, convenience foods, and many other examples of, in the words of Wiedemann and his colleagues, "the marketization of products and services which used to be provisioned through more time-intensive commons or reciprocal social arrangements."[84] And the society-wide system of overproduction and overconsumption is geared to increasing the wealth of a few.

When their returns on investment in the material world—that is, production and consumption—decline, the wealthy turn to the financial world, where money itself generates more money, without any goods or services produced. The emergence of blockchain-based cryptocurrencies—with the pioneering exchanges in Bitcoin and Ethereum at the time of this writing still dominant—have boiled the process down even further. These coding innovations appear to exist only for creating and exchanging digital assets in a decentralized network that is ostensibly unconnected to the physical world and answerable to no central authority anywhere. Despite the allure of a world without banks, the ecological impact of Bitcoin and other assets derived from it is huge and growing.

The impact lies in the digital "mining" of some cryptocurrencies, which requires extraordinarily complex, high-speed mathematical problem-solving by networks of powerful computers. The energy suck involved for processing such digital wealth is eye-popping. In a sample calculation, the cryptocurrency expert Alex de Vries reports that at a value of $42,000 per Bitcoin, the currency's rate of energy consumption is similar to that of all of the data-processing centers in the world combined. The resulting rate of emissions—90 million metric tons of carbon dioxide per year—is roughly equal to the London metropolitan area's rate of greenhouse-gas emissions from all sources.[85] As Bitcoin value increases beyond $42,000 per unit, negative environmental impact increases accordingly. And that's only Bitcoin. Including the impacts of all of its up-and-coming cryptocurrency competitors would add another 50 percent to the total energy consumption and emissions.

As Bitcoin-based assets attract more investors and processing demands intensify, more energy will be required to power the crypto financial system, increasing emissions. The Association for Computing Machinery explains the runaway feedback loop that follows:

> The result is a vicious cycle, with the potential to consume an increasing amount of electricity. More and more computing power is needed to mine bitcoin, which requires more and more electricity. ASICs [integrated circuits specialized for crypto work] can be used to supercharge your mining, which uses even more electricity, and if bitcoin's price rises, it becomes even more profitable to mine, which causes more miners to jump into the game. The more miners, the more computing power needed to crack bitcoin's math problems. And so the cycle begins anew.[86]

Not all cryptoassets require the same amount of processing power as do those based on Bitcoin's protocols. But *all* resources consumed by their underlying infrastructure, regardless of technical efficiency, amount to pure waste. "It's a pyramid scheme," said economist Tendayi Kapfidze about Bitcoin at the beginning of 2020. "It has no real utility in the world. They've been trying to create a [use] for it for ten years now. It's a solution in search of a problem and it still hasn't found a problem to solve."[87] "In the near term," reported the *New York Times* in March 2021, "nearly two-thirds of all Bitcoin mining is taking place in China, and 'mining activities can also be found in regions with coal-heavy power generation, such as in the province of Inner Mongolia,' according to a study in the scientific journal Joule, which also raises the idea of imposing a carbon tax. 'Regulating this largely gambling-driven source of carbon emissions appears to be a simple means to contribute to decarbonizing the economy.'"[88]

Whether or not cryptocurrencies are here to stay, it's up to each of us to insist that throughout the economy, money and material resources be put to their highest and most essential use, so that they help, not hurt, our prospects for securing a livable future.

There was much speculation in 2020–2021 that lessons could be learned from the pandemic experience that could be applied to climate. There were some obvious pragmatic lessons, for example, that it's possible to deeply reduce commuting, air travel, and international trade, and that more food needs to be grown locally. There was hope not only that the pandemic would permanently reduce carbon footprints but that it would change forever the nature of work. The latter prospect, however, applied only to certain jobs, largely in the services sector and disproportionately held by white medium-to-high earners. Working with colleagues, presentations at business meetings, and attendance at international conferences can be done via screens and speakers, whether or not those activities are necessary. Harvesting tomatoes, serving grocery customers, repairing plumbing, or caring for the sick or elderly—all considered essential work—cannot. Working from home is a privilege not enjoyed by the people who keep society running.

As countries become wealthier, surpassing the point at which they have resources and workforces adequate to satisfy the entire population's material needs, they increase the share of jobs in the service sector, which includes activities such as insurance, advertising, restaurant work, software development, education, and so on. There persists a widespread misconception that as a nation becomes wealthier and services occupy a larger and larger portion of its economy, increases in total wealth will have smaller and smaller impacts on resource use and climate. That will happen, the thinking goes, because a smaller share of the economy is being carried out in "dirty" factories, construction sites, trucking lines, farmers' fields, etc.

The vision of "clean" growth through a services economy is a mirage. Until recently, typical analyses failed to account for resources expended to maintain and support the key factor of production in service industries: the workers themselves. Every sector of the economy depends on the personal consumption that sustains its own workforce, and that consumption has ecological impacts. Logically, each industry should be charged with the ecological impacts of its own employees' personal consumption of both domestically produced and imported goods.

When emissions generated by its own employees as consumers are accounted for, the service sector's share of global carbon emissions more than doubles, from 22 to 45 percent. Services' impacts on land use and water consumption leap from 15 to almost 50 percent. And because people who make higher wages and salaries tend to generate greater quantities of greenhouse gases in their nonworking time, higher-wage industries in the service sector—such as "computers and related activities," public administration, and research and development—show much higher emissions and resource consumption than low-wage service industries. For example, total emissions from the subsector "computers and related activities" were twenty-five times as large as those of the lower-wage hotel and restaurant industries combined.

The researchers who performed these analyses found that "industries typically labelled 'dirty'...are not the main drivers of environmental pressures, and are also no 'dirtier' than services, which are typically thought of as high productivity sectors with low environmental burdens. Instead, we find that all sectors are roughly equivalent." To the researchers, the consequences were clear: "The scope for absolute economy–environment decoupling is considerably more limited than is typically assumed. Based on our analysis, we argue that the environmental burden of high-wage, labor-intensive...industries has been significantly understated."[89]

Discussing labor within officially designated categories omits a large share of care work. Whereas the service sector recognizes paid (often poorly paid) care work in, for example, education, child care, elder care, nursing, and cleaning work, economics ignore much labor of a similar nature that has not been commodified (and is largely feminized). Advocates for an economy that stays within ecological limits are stressing that this must change, that care work, most of which fills essential needs while having a light ecological impact, must play a pivotal role in the economy and be valued accordingly. In particular, care work—sustaining not only fellow humans but the Earth's ecological health—is a key element in the provision of universal basic services and should be prioritized at the same time that production of nonessential goods and services is being deeply reduced. In its broader context, Aubrey Streit Krug has written,

Care work is often rendered invisible and taken for granted....To learn new ways of caring for other beings—or remember ways that others have known but we have forgotten—some humans may first need to *un*learn. For instance, members of the dominant society in the US will need to let go of and dismantle certain things in order to care for the ecosphere. They will need to let go of the denial of crisis and harm, to let go of the domination of fellow non-humans and humans, to dismantle current systems and structures that actively reinforce domination and undermine the potential for equitable care, and to return homelands and make reparations to the Indigenous Peoples of the continent.[90]

As we strive to achieve a healthy, just, ecologically sustainable society, we know what's not going to work: technological fixes in energy, medicine, or agriculture; more intensive exploitation of land and labor; a bigger economic pie; an ostensibly "clean" services economy that values production over care. Those are dead ends. What is needed is the opposite: a society-wide, indeed a world-wide, commitment and strategy to restrain human activity within strict ecological limits. And this must be carried out in ways that involve leadership from all communities, particularly those traditionally left out of the decision-making process. The goal must be to achieve an impact on the Earth light enough that sufficiency and justice for all can be sustained through the coming chaotic decades and far beyond.

3.

A TO-DO LIST FOR THE 2020s

It is well known that 80 percent of the world's biodiversity exists within recognized Indigenous lands and territories. In addition, the IPCC [Intergovernmental Panel on Climate Change] has also recognized carbon sinks are often located on Indigenous lands and territories. This is not happenstance, but is the result of millennia of stewardship founded in deep, spiritual connections with our lands and territories and not predicated on modern economic systems.
—Indigenous Climate Action, 2019[91]

DISASTERS THE SIZE of the whole Earth, several of which are now raging all at once, require a cooperative international response. No international agreements—the toothless 2015 Paris Climate Agreement included—have proven capable of rising to the challenges we now face. One thing we have learned from three decades of failed global climate negotiations is that there can be no effective global action as long as individual nation-states fail to take action on their own. Nations will have to adopt their own very ambitious climate goals and policies in order to lay the foundation for international coordination. National policies will also provide umbrellas under which local communities can take action, keeping the whole effort just, equitable, and small-d democratic.

Under the failed leadership of Team Trump, Washington totally bungled its response to the cascading events of 2020, in everything from public health to human rights, the environment and the economy. Despite countless vigorous efforts, it was beyond the power of state and local governments, civil society, or individuals to compensate fully for the White House's repeated sabotage of national policies that could have averted much suffering, death, and racialized abuse. Similarly, any nation will fail to do its part to end the climate emergency unless its government takes decisive action to abolish greenhouse emissions and helps society equitably adapt to the economic consequences. The U.S. government failed to do anything like that, and as a result we emerged from 2020 as the world's worst miscreant in both public health and climate.

Vigorous national action alone, while essential, is not sufficient to resolve either the public health or the climatic crises we will continue to face. We learned the hard way that when an emergency as dangerous as the Covid-19 pandemic is not met with both decisive leadership in Washington and unprecedented actions on the ground in communities, workplaces, and households, failure is certain. This same principle has long been exemplified by our failure to address the climate emergency. Can a national umbrella policy for the fair and just elimination of fossil fuels, accompanied by local, democratic management of resource allocation, work as a single, seamless system while also serving as part of a global system for getting rid of fossil fuels? Can similar policies rescue local, national, and global food systems?

NATIONALIZE THIS!

THERE IS GROWING awareness that we must stop using oil, gas, and coal, and that doing so will require that fossil fuels be removed from market control. The fuel industries and their oil, gas, and coal reserves must, therefore, be nationalized. In a 2020 white paper titled "Out of Time: The Case for Nationalizing the Fossil Fuel Industry," a group of scholars in energy and economics laid out a tight, convincing case that a public takeover of all fuels is the only way "to overcome many of the systemic hurdles that prevent meaningful action, allowing us to move towards decarbonization in a way that is planned, provides for workers, and supports communities."[92] The authors were writing during the early days of the pandemic, when the dollar value of fossil fuels had crashed. Anticipating that prices would remain low for years, they suggested that the U.S. government could buy out the industries and ensure a just transition for their workers (but not for their executives and investors), at bargain prices with money borrowed at historically low interest rates.

Nationalization will be necessary because fossil-fuel industry executives, knowing full well the role their products have played in triggering catastrophic warming of the Earth, continue to deceive the public while pumping, mining, processing, and selling fuels at handsome profits. The companies are committed to this course of action and could not cease and desist even if they wanted to; as the authors put it, "Their heavy investments in fossil fuel reserves, extraction, and transport means that they need to keep extracting and selling to the market for decades to come to recoup the costs of the capital-intensive infrastructure." (U.S. electric utilities are certainly counting on the persistence of fossil fuels; they are planning to build a staggering 235 new natural gas–fired power stations in coming years.[93]) The oil and gas companies will continue to use their vaunted political power to resist all efforts to reduce their output. If fossil fuels are to be kicked out of the economy for good, the authors of "Out of Time" argue, they must be nationalized; furthermore, they urge, extraction and use of the fuels must be reduced at a rate of 6 percent per year until we are finally and completely free of them.

There is ample historical precedent for nationalization around the world and even in the United States. During World Wars I and II, the government was compelled to take control of critical resources and industries: coal mines, meatpacking plants, shipyards, railways, the telegraph system, and much more. Unable to convince manufacturers to scale up production of essential goods, or to stop expending scarce resources on production of nonessential goods, Washington had no choice but to nationalize factories. The "Out of Time" authors point out other cases of nationalization in the immediate postwar years, as well as the government takeover of more than 1,000 savings and loan institutions during the scandal-ridden financial crisis of the late 1980s and early 1990s. They argue that in the current century, the simplest way to nationalize would be for the Federal Reserve to simply buy a majority share in every fossil fuel company. At the time they were writing, the entire industry was valued at about $700 billion, making the buyout much more affordable than the corporate bailouts handed out during the Great Recession and Covid-19 pandemic. In fact, it should be easy, at that price, to have a forced buyout of the whole industry rather than just buying a majority share. That would avoid endless conflict with minority shareholders.

Nationalization and a rapid decrease of the fossil fuel supply would have to be accompanied by policies to protect workers in the oil, gas, and coal industries as well as energy consumers throughout society. This "just transition" will require creation of good new jobs in other sectors for workers currently in fossil fuel and related industries, along with retraining and social support. The authors note that "not every job lost will be matched by a job created at the same location," but that geographical mismatch can be evened out by fostering new employment in all marginalized communities and economically disadvantaged regions, whatever the cause of their economic stress. The just transition will also require the restoration of landscapes and waters that have been ruined by extraction of fuels, and the return of those lands and waters to Indigenous communities from whom they were stolen. It will require dismantling of refineries, power plants, and all the rest of the vast infrastructure that processes and transports fuels, and remediating the air, land, and water that has contaminated the people surrounding the refineries—most often communities of color and first-generation immigrants.

If it's to be accomplished quickly enough, the phase-out of fossil fuels has to occur simultaneously with, and move faster than, the development of new energy sources and infrastructure. Therefore, the phase-out must be accompanied by systems to ensure that communities are protected from energy shortages. That will require much more equitable access to energy. Today, more affluent, predominantly white households have much higher than average consumption of energy in all forms, while millions of lower-income households cannot afford as much energy as they need. Just as market forces are unable to reduce the supply of fossil fuels at the source, they are powerless to ensure that some businesses and households don't hog the diminishing energy supply while other workers and consumers cannot get access to a share of energy sufficient to get to their jobs or keep the heat and lights on at home. Here, where the market fails, fair-shares rationing must bridge the gap.

UNDER THE UMBRELLA

RATIONING IS NOT a means of reducing fossil fuel consumption or greenhouse emissions. That's going to have to be accomplished with a declining cap on total fuel supplies. Rationing is instead an adaptation to that reduced supply, ensuring sufficiency and fairness. According to the foundational ecological economist Herman Daly, a society successfully living within ecological limits has to have rules that can achieve each of the society's goals, and each of the rules has to be "nested" within all higher-priority rules. He has argued that, to succeed, a sustainable economy must obey rules of scale, distribution, and allocation, in that order of priority. Briefly, the *maximum scale* of the economy's material input and waste output first must be etched in stone, so to speak. Then rules for distribution must be established such that essential goods and services are produced in sufficient quantities and that *equitable access* to them is assured. But crucially, the distribution rules cannot violate the scale rules. That prohibits, for example, increasing the size of the resource pie in order to increase the size of the smaller slices. Instead, distortions in access to resources must be eliminated. Once scale and distribution rules are being strictly and fairly followed, Daly argues, goods and services can then be allocated by buying and selling.[94]

Imagine that someday soon the United States nationalizes the fossil fuel industries; that a cap is placed on extraction and use of oil, gas, and coal; and that the cap declines briskly year to year, thereby imposing, in Daly's terms, the proper scale. Progressive economic policies, enforcement of equality and justice, rationing, price controls, and a just transition away from fossil fuels could ensure equitable access to energy, and they would have to be designed so that they did not violate the cap on total extraction and consumption. So far, so good for scale and distribution. However, if allocation of the diminishing supplies of fuels is left up to the market as envisioned in Daly's nested economy, the result is all too predictable. Not only will we see blackouts and endless queueing at gas stations, but there will be too many private jets in the air and too little public transportation on the ground, too many electric cars sucking from the grid and not enough electricity to keep the lights on in apartment buildings, too many yachts in the Caribbean and not enough staple foods on store shelves. One of the most critical needs is to have all electric power generation become the exclusive domain of democratically run public utilities, with all of them linked to a national grid and a cooperative management network. The long-standing need to have electricity under control of the people and not corporations became blindingly obvious when the deep freeze of February 2021 triggered a power-grid crash that crippled the state of Texas. In a society that aims to end greenhouse warming, energy and other resources must be allocated not where they will generate the most profit but where they will meet the most important human needs. Seen in this light, the path to a livable future is clearly not going to be a capitalist one. That might be hard for some to imagine, but it doesn't have to be. "We live in capitalism," wrote Ursula K. LeGuin: "Its power seems inescapable." But, she reminds us, "So did the divine right of kings. Any human power can be resisted and changed by human beings."

Non-market national policies for allocation of energy supplies among industries, and fair-shares rationing among households have been proposed (see the Climate Mobilization's "Victory Plan" and Larry Edwards's and my "Cap and Adapt" framework[95]), and historical experience suggests that such policies would succeed in containing society's ecological impact within required limits. But while the legislation for a policy such as Cap and Adapt would be written and passed by elected representatives, with ample input from constituents, they would by necessity be top-down interventions that apply nationwide. Otherwise, the proper scale of resource use would almost certainly be exceeded. Therefore, to be broadly accepted, these policies would also need to allow plenty of room for community decision-making, in the form of what has come to be called deliberative democracy.

An umbrella of nationwide rules limiting total quantities of fossil fuels and providing for their fair allocation would change the means by which the fuels are dealt with at street level in counties, cities, and neighborhoods. Today, fuels are traded as private goods; you compete with other customers for them, and you get as much or as little as you pay for. But with nationalization and Cap and Adapt, fossil fuels would be treated instead as if they were what economists call "common-pool resources," meaning that consumption by one person or business leaves a smaller quantity for others to consume, while no consumers may be barred access to the good.

For decades, the Nobel Prize–winning economist Elinor Ostrom and colleagues have studied common-pool resources from the standpoint that "forests, water systems, fisheries, and the global atmosphere are all common-pool resources of immense importance for the survival of humans on this earth." They studied a wide range of community efforts to govern the distribution of common-pool resources and came up with a set of "design principles" that could improve the odds of a successful effort. Rules for sharing the resource, for example, must conform to local social and ecological conditions. Those who are affected by the rules must be the ones who make the rules and also monitor the resource and its use. Sanctions for those who violate the rules should start out mild but become harsher with repeated violations. Modest, friendly arenas for conflict resolution must be created to provide ample opportunity for face-to-face communication. Finally, and crucially, community control of the common-pool resource should be compatible with regional and national efforts—in Ostrom's words, it should be "closely connected to a larger social-ecological system," with governance "organized in multiple nested layers."[96]

We don't have to invent from scratch such local, nested, deliberative, democratic processes for allocating scarce energy and other resources in accord with national policy. There are plenty of precedents for local administration of scarce resources.[97]

GROUNDED DEMOCRACY

THE IDEA OF participatory budgeting has been around a long time, but the experience of the southern Brazilian city of Porto Alegre from the late 1980s into the early 2000s was an inspiration for thousands of such experiments around the world. In brief, the city government put the drafting of each year's budget for all public capital expenditure—functions like street repairs and improvements, water supplies and sanitation, health care, and development of green space— in the hands of the city's residents. The process involved a complex year-long cycle that included neighborhood meetings for ranking priorities, the election of delegates to area and citywide councils that drew up the budget, and a monitoring committee to ensure that improvements were carried out as planned. The mayor and city council had final say on the budget approval, but they generally made only minor revisions to the budgets they received, because they would have to answer in future elections to the very voters who had developed the budget.[98]

Participatory budgeting in Porto Alegre grew out of the city's long history of neighborhood and workplace activism. Most of the participants were from marginalized communities, largely because their neighborhoods had the greatest need for improvement of basic services. The process, however, was vulnerable to partisan political changes. In 2004, a less progressive party came to power in the city and slashed the portion of capital funds subject to bottom-up budgeting, thereby gutting the entire process. But at least by that time, thanks in large part to participatory budgeting, Porto Alegre's residents had gained universal access to ample water, sanitation, green space, and other elements of a good quality of life.[99]

Most participatory budgeting efforts that followed in other cities around the world have been more limited in scope and impact. Nevertheless, there are good recent examples of the process in allocating funds for environmental action in New York City, Lisbon, Brussels, and elsewhere. Analogous forms of participatory allocation in the local management of energy and physical resources could be important in a low-energy future.

The group Black Lives Matter Los Angeles has used broad-based participatory processes to develop a "People's Budget"[100] that would meet the city's needs far better than the existing budget, in which more than half of all funds go to the police department. (At the time of this writing, the People's Budget remains a grassroots proposal; the city has not yet adopted a participatory budgeting procedure.)

In their 2020–2021 budget, city residents called for allocating 47 percent of all funds to "universal aid and crisis management," which included housing, renters' support, food assistance, job-hunting assistance, public health care, youth development, climate mitigation and adaptation, environmental protection, and—as is appropriate for a notoriously fire- and earthquake-prone city—disaster preparedness. The "built environment" budget, accounting for 28 percent of total funding, would go to cover physical infrastructure, including public transportation, libraries, parks, public works, and fire protection. Another 25 percent was for "community safety services," some of which are currently under the control of law enforcement. They include family counseling, restorative justice programs, reparations, community events, community-led crisis response, and response to gang and domestic violence without police involvement. Finally, just 1.6 percent of the budget would go to traditional law enforcement, including police, traffic enforcement, and the city attorney's office.

In a statement accompanying the budget, BLM-LA explained, "When deciding how to allocate resources, the question becomes who and what do we value most: Is it investing in our children, providing shelter, food, and medical care for our most vulnerable populations? Is it helping our city withstand a global pandemic? Or is it investing in a police state that won't make our communities any safer, and will actually harm those who need help the most, especially now? "[101] Clearly, the adoption of participatory budgeting would turn Los Angeles into a very different city, especially if the proposed restriction of the policing budget is supported by federal legislation to end state-sanctioned violence. The George Floyd Justice in Policing Act, passed by the U.S. House in March, 2021, would have banned chokeholds, outlaw racial profiling, restrict the use of no-knock warrants, create a nationwide police-misconduct database, and weaken "qualified immunity," making it easier for plaintiffs to sue police for violating their rights.[102] Despite the George Floyd bill's laudable provisions, the national network Movement for Black Lives opposed it on the grounds that it did not go far enough. They advocated for legislation that would not only end qualified immunity but also abolish mandatory minimum and life sentences and divert law-enforcement and incarceration funding to communities for use in dealing with systemic racial injustice.[103]

Another example of local deliberative democracy is the formation of citizens' assemblies: large groups of residents that meet to study and deliberate over public policy issues and then make recommendations or decisions. Composition of the assemblies is determined by a process known as sortition, with members being computer-selected at random to form a statistically representative sample of the population with respect to age, ethnicity, income, community, and other factors. Assemblies spend many hours hearing factual testimony on the issues at hand from all angles, engage in discussion, and report their decisions. From 2006 to 2020, at least 120 citizens' assemblies were formed in at least twenty countries around the world. Each deliberated over one or more issues that reached into many areas of public life, including democratic reforms, nuclear energy, health care, mental illness, housing, air pollution, biometrics, Brexit, and climate policy. Perhaps most famously, the process leading to legalization of abortion in Ireland began with a citizens' assembly. Advocates of assemblies say that the groups' random yet inclusive makeup and fact-finding orientation minimizes influences that plague elected governmental bodies, such as big money, conflicts of interest, and bigotry, while ensuring all communities are represented.[104]

Citizens' assemblies need to be free to deliberate independently of government influence, or else they will falter. As a case in point, in late 2020, Scotland's Parliament created a citizens' assembly to address the question "How should Scotland change to tackle the climate emergency in a fair and effective way?" More than one hundred citizens were randomly selected to represent the diversity of Scotland's population. Their deliberations, moved online because of the pandemic, carried on for seven Saturdays and Sundays, with eight hours spent each weekend. A member of Extinction Rebellion who was in the "stewarding group" that helped form the assembly wrote that such processes are a good way to deal with a fraught issue like climate, because "in response to the climate emergency we, as a society, have to navigate between the need to be 'political realists'—aware of how radical action on the climate could severely disrupt everyday life and business as usual—and 'physics realists'— aware of the need to transform the system if we are not to unleash catastrophic ecological unravelling."[105] Unfortunately, government representatives serving in the stewarding group steered its climate target toward a leisurely reduction of greenhouse emissions that would be far too slow to stop catastrophic warming. Declaring that the assembly was "in danger of becoming little more than a glorified focus group," both of the stewarding group's Extinction Rebellion members resigned.

Participatory budgeting and citizens' assemblies are focused locally, but we can imagine such practices being the foundation of a large-scale system for resource sufficiency and conservation "organized in multiple nested layers," as Ostrom proposed. On this, there may be lessons to draw from the longstanding American tradition of Soil and Water Conservation Districts. Created under the New Deal in the 1930s, the districts were organized to prevent soil erosion and protect local water quality by adopting and enforcing regulations and carrying out conservation projects on and around farmers' land, with federal funding and oversight. Today, fully 99 percent of U.S. farms lie within a district. Democratic forms of governance are central. Members of their boards of supervisors are elected by residents of the district, and all regulations or ordinances proposed by the board must be approved by residents by referendum. The districts are federally created entities, so they receive funding directly from Washington to carry out conservation projects, and in both projects and enforcement, they operate independently of state and local governments. However, because board members deal directly with local residents, many of whom they know well, they have been far more active in facilitating projects than in enforcing regulations on their neighbors.[106]

Multilayered administration of scarce resources is a central feature of the health care system in Cuba. With its small *consultarios* staffed by a doctor and a nurse in every neighborhood and each such clinic being integrated into a national system of public hospitals and outpatient polyclinics (*policlínicos integrales*), Cuba has achieved health outcomes in life expectancy and infant mortality that rank it alongside the world's wealthiest countries. With a health system integrated from neighborhood to national scale, the island was well prepared for the Covid-19 pandemic. The government quickly turned school uniform factories to the task of manufacturing medical masks. They barred all nonresident travel to and from the island, temporarily sacrificing the tourism industry on which the economy depended, at the peak of the season. They locked down virus hot spots, ensuring that residents of those neighborhoods were well provisioned on a daily basis and that medically vulnerable people were monitored and cared for frequently. They thoroughly tested and sought out those who had been in contact with infected people. Medical students made the rounds of all neighborhoods on foot, checking in on the residents.[107]

The same high degree of social organization that underlay the public health system's successful response to Covid-19 has also earned the nation a sterling reputation in this greenhouse century for successful hurricane preparedness and response, and for strong rebuilding efforts following major storms. Death tolls from climatic disasters are very low compared with those experienced by other Caribbean islands, including Puerto Rico. Citizens organize systematically for preparedness, cleanup, and rebuilding, even training children as young as nine years old; in advance of hurricane landfall, they flag all households and family members who need assistance with their evacuation.

RATIONING AT GROUND LEVEL

THE MOST APT historical precedent for local administration of national limits on resource use may be the World War II–era allocation of goods in the United States by local rationing boards under a national umbrella. Allocation of energy and other resources between the civilian and military economies and within the civilian economy was centrally determined by the War Production Board, and national regulations for price controls and rationing were set by the federal Office of Price Administration. Management of civilian allocation in communities, on the other hand, was carried out by approximately 5,600 local rationing boards. The Office of Price Administration entitled every household in the country to a standard ration of essential goods; in addition, consumers could apply for supplemental rations of some of those goods. The universal distribution of standard rations, as well as the allocation of supplemental rations to applicants who could demonstrate the greatest need, was carried out by the local boards. Most of the decisions on allocation of supplemental rations facing the boards involved energy sources, primarily gasoline and heating oil.

Board members were volunteers. They were guided by a constantly updated "loose-leaf manual" of regulations from the national rationing office, but as long as they did not exceed their federally assigned monthly quotas, they enjoyed a high degree of discretion in responding to applications. Indeed, one observer wrote that boards could be "as much influenced by non-legal circumstances as a jury in a negligence case."[108] When applicants were dissatisfied with decisions, the strict quotas handed down from Washington provided board members with a degree of cover; they could say, "We're sorry, but we just haven't been allotted enough this month for you to get extra coupons." This was essential to the boards' gaining broad if sometimes grudging acceptance of the restraints under which society was obliged to operate at the time. The rationing boards focused on ensuring that all families received their fair shares of essential goods.

Like soil conservation district boards, they were often understandably reluctant to carry out their other assignments, which involved enforcing regulations against food hoarding or black-market trafficking of rationed goods. Those committing such offenses were, after all, members of the board members' own community.

In a history of wartime rationing written for the Office of Price Administration, Emmette Redford noted that the very existence of a board composed of community members "was the most effective means of obtaining favorable community sentiment."[109] The boards, however, were not genuinely democratic institutions. Members were appointed by federal administrators, not elected. By law, each board was to be representative of its community, and overall, with respect to gender, class, and occupation, they were. However, this was still the Jim Crow era. Nationally, a minuscule 0.7 percent of board members were Black, with a good share of them serving on segregated all-Black boards in the Southeast.

In a future where fossil fuels are being eliminated and energy is allocated to industrial sectors and rationed to households, ration allowances and rules would need to be set nationally, as they were during World War II. However, thanks to digital technology, the mechanics of energy rationing in the future would be much less laborious than it was back when wartime boards had the onerous task of distributing books of paper stamps and coupons to all residents. For the sake of acceptance and justice, however, implementation should not be wholly hierarchical and automated. Although basic household rations should be uniform nationwide, some local discretion could be achieved by allocating to each community an additional pool of collective fuel and electricity rations to be allocated for the common good through deliberative democratic processes. In the World War 2–era precedent, local boards issued extra fuel coupons to households or businesses that needed them; in future energy rationing, the supplemental quotas could be designated for the collective good, with a focus on historically disadvantaged communities. For local governance of energy rationing, the federal government could, for example, foster the creation of self-organizing community cooperatives that would oversee but not control the process. Participation would be open to all and representative of the community in all its dimensions. Deliberations over energy resources should include voices from all sectors of the community and have as a top goal to make reparations for past inequities in access to resources. For making the process reparative, Black Lives Matter L.A.'s People's Budget provides a good example. Porto Alegre's participatory budgeting system is another. It had roots in existing neighborhood-based social movements and was aimed primarily at providing and improving basic services and infrastructure in low-income and marginalized communities, and the process was carried out largely by members of those communities.

Rationing of residential electricity use would raise some interesting dilemmas. For example, until a massive, federally funded installation of community wind and solar capacity could be established in low-income and marginalized neighborhoods, disparities in energy access could be worsened under rationing. If some homeowners, for example, invest in rooftop solar arrays, inverters, and batteries in order to supplement their basic electricity rations, then the more affluent, largely white households who disproportionately install rooftop solar today could buy their way out of the limit on electricity consumption set by the ration. To prevent this potential inequity, all household solar-generation systems could be required by law to be connected to the power grid; in return, owners would receive monetary credits from the utility for the power they feed into the grid (as in so-called "feed-in tariff" systems). They would, in effect, become part of the public electric utility, increasing the pool of energy available to all, and being paid for what they produce. For purposes of equity, however, their own total consumption would be limited to the standard electricity ration that applies to all households.

A nationwide policy to install publicly funded rooftop or community solar arrays in lower-income communities would further increase the pool of electricity and increase the standard ration available to all households. Local, collective coordination under a national umbrella could also make access to energy fairer and more secure. This could be crucial in marginalized areas. Puerto Rico may be heading in that direction. Despite the Trump administration's malign neglect of the island in the years following Hurricane Maria, its residents have made progress in creating a more resilient electric power system. Maria took down almost 850 transmission towers and 50,000 distribution poles. An estimated 80 percent of power lines came down. Two months after the storm, 60 percent of Puerto Rico's residents remained in the dark. Researchers have since been proposing less centralized, more resilient electric grids featuring clusters of approximately ten households, each setting up its own solar photovoltaic system with battery storage. These "microgrids" would be fully integrated with the island-wide power system, but whenever the supply from power plants is cut off, the microgrids could keep producing in isolation.[110] Steps have been taken toward such a system, and in the year and a half following Maria, the number of rooftop solar installations doubled, to 4 percent of electric capacity.

Even with a Cap and Adapt–type system, with national energy limits, rationing, price controls, and local discretion, many economically stressed households may be unable to afford their full share of fuel or electricity, or may have to spend too large a portion of their income to obtain their share. Policies like those proposed to address the Covid-19 pandemic and as part of a Green New Deal would be required: income and housing guarantees, universal basic services (including health care), home insulation campaigns, extensive development of free, safe public transportation, and others.

GLOBAL CLIMATE JUSTICE

WHILE COMMUNITY AND regional governance of resources should occur under a national umbrella that guarantees both limits and fair shares, the national effort must in turn connect to an international mobilization. Otherwise, humanity's total emissions can't be driven down to zero in time. Therefore, once the United States begins turning off the national fossil-fuel tap and pursues a just transition, with local governance ensuring fairness and equity, Washington can begin forming alliances with other countries that also commit to direct elimination of fossil fuels. At that point, we would land right in the thick of a nascent global movement that's pressing for a "Fossil Fuel Nonproliferation Treaty." Recognizing that the Paris Agreement is utterly incapable of preventing runaway atmospheric warming, advocates for a nonproliferation treaty want to create what would in essence be a global version of Cap and Adapt. The treaty would be modeled explicitly on the Nuclear Nonproliferation Treaty that was put forward in the 1960s and has been signed by almost all the world's nations. Whereas the nuclear treaty required nations to agree never to develop nuclear weapons, the fuel treaty would require nations to agree to leave most of their fossil fuel reserves in the ground forever. The nuclear treaty required disarmament: This new treaty would provide for dismantlement of the infrastructure that enables fossil fuel extraction and use. The nuclear treaty provided assistance for "peaceful" development of nuclear energy capacity to states that agreed not to develop weapons: The fuel treaty would provide funds and technology for renewable energy development, through a "Global Transition Fund" that would help low-income countries supply their energy needs without dependence on oil, gas, and coal.[111]

Citing the example of yet another landmark treaty, the Chemical Weapons Convention, advocates for a Fossil Fuel Nonproliferation Treaty foresee provisions for "mutual verified compliance" among nation-states, through independent accounting of oil, gas, and coal reserves and production, with monitoring and inspection. They note that the "upstream" nature of the controls (aimed directly at the wellhead and mine), along with the relatively concentrated ownership of most of the world's fossil fuel reserves and infrastructure, would make global accounting much simpler, more accurate, and far less open to lying and cheating than controls have proven to be in carbon emissions trading systems. In 2021, the Dalai Lama and one hundred other Nobel laureates in peace, literature, medicine, physics, chemistry, and economics signed a letter giving the treaty fullthroated support, declaring:

> Leaders, not industry, hold the power and have the moral responsibility to take bold actions to address this crisis. We call on world leaders to work together in a spirit of international cooperation to:
>
> - End new expansion of oil, gas and coal production in line with the best available science…;
>
> - Phase out existing production of oil, gas and coal in a manner that is fair and equitable, taking into account the responsibilities of countries for climate change and their respective dependency on fossil fuels, and capacity to transition;
>
> - Invest in a transformational plan to ensure 100% access to renewable energy globally, support dependent economies to diversify away from fossil fuels, and enable people and communities across the globe to flourish through a global just transition.[112]

The thorniest issue, given the huge disparities among countries in their quantities of fuel reserves, their energy needs, and their economic status, is the question of burden sharing. How could the treaty determine, for such disparate nations, their permitted fuel extraction and required rates of reduction? Treaty advocates Peter Newell and Andrew Simms of Sussex University have suggested three principles: that the burden of action should be borne primarily by wealthier nations; that nations creating the most greenhouse gas emissions from their own fossil fuel reserves should act first; and that emissions should be reduced most rapidly by nations that have the greatest historical use of fossil fuels.[113] Based on those criteria, they recommend that the wealthy nations of the Organization for Economic Cooperation and Development (OECD) plus Russia take the lead in setting short-term targets and timetables, and start phasing out fossil fuels quickly. Next would come large countries with high current emissions but much less historic responsibility for climate change, such as China, India, Brazil, and Indonesia. Finally, meeting fossil fuel reduction targets in low-emitting, low-income countries, they write, will depend on lots of international aid to build up their non-fossil energy capacity and meet other development needs.

Any effort to come to global agreement on eliminating fossil fuels involves an international analogue to our domestic just transition: What to do about the nations around the world, from Nigeria to Ecuador, that are deeply dependent on revenue generated by fossil fuels for maintaining their people's living standards and preventing widespread poverty. The nonprofit groups Oil Change International and Stockholm Environment Institute have declared, "The need for a just transition—and the management of other social costs—should be taken into account to determine not the pace of transition [which must be fast], but the manner in which it is implemented and the resources devoted to it. Neither driving a rapid transition, nor making it just, should be used as an excuse for not delivering on the other."[114] Principles of environmental justice, they write, dictate that fossil fuel extraction should be ended first and fastest where local communities and their environments are harmed by fossil fuel extraction more than they are helped by the use or sale of the fuels. The next criterion would be to reduce extraction most rapidly where dependence on fossil fuels for jobs or tax revenue is low, and after that, where economies and institutions have the highest capacity to absorb the costs and difficulties of the transition away from fossil fuels.

Achieving global adoption of any agreement to end fossil-fuel extraction is a daunting prospect. To get around the typical "You go first!"/"No, you go first!" standoffs among high-emitting nations, some treaty supporters are suggesting, as I have above, that smaller alliances of nations ("clubs") get together to work out their own joint fossil-fuel reduction plans as a proof of concept, and then at some point clubs and nations could coalesce into a movement toward a global nonproliferation treaty.

BEYOND FOSSIL FUELS

THE ORIGINAL Cap and Adapt proposal was tightly aimed at one threat to the Earth: greenhouse gases coming from one source, fossil fuels. Freeing ourselves from fossil fuels will have the additional benefit of augmenting society's ability to undertake activities with less ecological damage. And whereas replacing electricity generation from fossil fuels currently requires mineral mining, industrial pollution, and widespread encroachment on ecosystems, most efforts to reduce greenhouse gases from direct burning of fossil fuels in transportation, agriculture, and manufacturing would be ecologically beneficial; they are in fact actions we should already be taking for other good reasons.

Freeing ourselves of fossil fuels will eliminate pollution that goes well beyond carbon emissions. Production of all sorts of harmful compounds will be hampered without free availability of petroleum. Leaving natural gas in the ground will be the surest way to stop the gas industry's leakage of methane, which accounts for almost 10 percent of total U.S. greenhouse emissions each year. With use of fossil fuels curtailed, smog will clear from cities; the paving of more and more acreage to accommodate vehicular traffic and aviation will, one hopes, become unnecessary; and the overall quality of urban life will improve immeasurably. Taking funds for buying petroleum products away from the Pentagon will not only slash carbon emissions but also curb the ecological and human destruction that the military inflicts in the course of its daily routine. In a smaller but welcome step, the cruise industry will be dismantled, barred forever from polluting the seas or exploiting the labor of crew members while it exposes them to potentially deadly outbreaks.

As the United States grapples with the necessity to reduce greenhouse emissions from all sources, we need to reboot the national discussion of essential versus nonessential goods and services that flared up during the pandemic peaks. We need a more serious debate over how to determine which products and services are essential; which are useful, with little harmful impact in their production or consumption and therefore might be produced if we have the resources; and which should be declared wasteful luxuries and banned. Our entangled ecological crises compel us to use less energy and reduce exploitation of resources and ecosystems by producing and importing less and limiting unnecessary services. That creates the need to differentiate between which goods and services (and how much of each) we need as individuals and as a society, and which we can do without if we can't afford to produce and use them in ways that are ecologically favorable. And the heavier a product's or service's environmental impact, the stricter the criteria should be for declaring it essential. As an example, I once again offer that near-ubiquitous feature of American life that hits the atmosphere with a serious one-two punch: air-conditioning.

As a heavy user of electricity, air-conditioning is responsible for large and growing emissions of carbon dioxide from coal-fired and natural gas–fired power plants. And among greenhouse gases that need to be eliminated, those of greatest concern (other than carbon dioxide and methane) include refrigerants used in freezers and refrigerators, heat pumps, and air-conditioning. All of the most widely used refrigerants—compounds capable of efficiently transferring heat out of a room or car or refrigerator—have very high global warming potential. There are efforts to prevent refrigerant leakage during manufacturing and running of the equipment and to recycle the compounds when the equipment is taken out of use. But those efforts can go only so far, and these gases cannot be kept contained forever; eventually, virtually all refrigerants that are produced end up contaminating and warming the atmosphere.

Unfortunately, there are no available refrigerants that avoid climate impact while also transferring heat efficiently and safely. Ammonia was long used in industrial refrigeration, but it is toxic and prone to fire and explosion. The same goes for propane. (You don't really want the refrigerant running through your air-conditioner to be the same chemical compound as the fuel running your barbecue grill.) Even carbon dioxide can be used as a refrigerant, but it's highly inefficient. In fact, none of these or other alternative refrigerants is as efficient as currently used, highly efficient, climate-unfriendly compounds, which results in a catch-22 situation. Cooling systems using climate-safe but less efficient refrigerants would consume more electricity per amount of cooling and thereby cause higher carbon emissions from the local power plant than would current systems. The total climatic impact could be greater than with today's refrigerants.

The most direct way to reduce emissions of refrigerants from air conditioners and refrigerators while also using less energy is to do a lot less cooling. Certainly, there is an amount of cooling that can be classified as essential. Recall that a small refrigerator for food preservation is listed as a necessary element of decent living standards globally, and that for vulnerable populations, air-conditioning can mean the difference between life and death during increasingly frequent and intense heat waves. Nevertheless, excessive nonessential use of air-conditioning—and, to a lesser extent, refrigeration—occurs worldwide, and most egregiously in the United States. Reducing the use of both will be requisite to keep greenhouse warming within tolerable limits. Refrigeration is a necessary part of modern life, but there is plenty of opportunity to reduce its use in the United States and some other affluent nations. Air-conditioning can of course help keep people alive under harsh conditions, and that is no small thing. Nevertheless, it is important to acknowledge that in that role, the air conditioner is an in-case-of-emergency-break-glass tool. It's not designed to fix the underlying social and economic injustices from which people under heat stress need to be rescued. And there are alternatives. In 2020, a group of researchers published a paper in which they used biophysical modeling to figure out how personal heat stress could be prevented while still allowing enough indoor ventilation to reduce spread of the coronavirus. They projected that in 95 out of the 105 largest U.S. cities, home to almost two-thirds of the population, open windows, electric fans, and, when needed, an occasional fine spray of water to the skin, can provide relief even during the most severe heat waves.[115]

OVERHAULING THE FOOD SYSTEM

THE U.S. FOOD producing and processing systems had already been an ecological and human rights disaster for decades when, in 2020, their owners and managers responded to the pandemic by further tightening the screws of exploitation. Heading into a future of dual climate and public health emergencies will require a deep transformation of the agriculture and food economies. The changes required to end the fragility of the food system and the vulnerability of its workers to infectious disease have long been desperately needed on broader humanitarian and environmental grounds.

The time has long passed to abolish feedlots for cattle, as well as confined feeding operations for swine, poultry, and other animals. Tens of millions of acres now being used to grow dent corn and soybeans for feeding cattle can be converted to pasture and hay production, and eventually to perennial food-grain/pasture crops. Both beef and dairy cattle should be allowed to eat what they were born to eat: grasses and forage legumes. Swine, poultry, and egg production should likewise be moved to "free-range" conditions, but they will still require feed grains. The meat-producing corporations must be broken up, with meat production and processing done on a small scale and regulated much more strictly for health and safety. Such measures would result in better but more limited national supplies of meat and poultry. That's not a problem. Deep reductions in consumption of animal products, especially factory-farmed meats, have long been recommended for nutritional and ecological concerns; their heavy environmental impact is especially prominent.

For fruits and vegetables, it is essential to stop and reverse the longstanding effort to speed up production in fields and food factories. A necessary first step is a federal guarantee that farmworkers (along with food processing workers, including in the meat industry) have the right to unionize. Food needs to be produced and processed at a humane, ecologically supportable pace that can guarantee workers' rights, safety, and economic security. Those goals can best be achieved if food is produced and processed chiefly by worker-owned cooperatives paying a living wage. That would bring an end to the farmworker paradox; finally, society's most essential workers would have income and working conditions that reflect their pivotal role in society.

As much fresh produce as possible should be grown close to the populations who will be eating them—whether on small truck farms or in community gardens and greenhouses. The resurgence of 1940s-style backyard "victory gardens" in response to pandemic-induced food shortages was a positive development that we can hope will keep expanding. Localizing vegetable production would not necessarily reduce the total output. Vegetables currently occupy only 3 percent of national cropland, so they could easily be dispersed among myriad small plots of land in every state and every community. What we'll no longer have, however, is access to every type of fresh vegetable and fruit any day of the year. We'll eat fresh whatever is in season and preserve vegetables for the off-season. The range of what is in season can be expanded. In northerly regions, vegetables can be grown in simple, inexpensive, unheated greenhouses almost year-round.[116] In summer and fall, home and community canning operations could make locally grown produce available all year, as they did in the war years of the 1940s. That would diversify the northerly vegetable diet in winter and spring.

Staple food grains, oilseeds, and dry beans and peas are compact, nonperishable foundations of the human diet; they—and products like flour that are made from them—are dry, have a long shelf lif, and can be shipped to every part of the country by rail with minimum energy use and carbon emissions. Such crops occupy a large proportion of U.S. cropland already, and, as the meat supply shrinks, more millions of acres of these crops will be needed. They must continue to be produced across vast swaths of rural America, mostly far from large metropolitan areas. But production should occur on numerous small farms, not the smaller and smaller numbers of ever-larger farms we see today. Furthermore, governments have to break the backs of the handful of huge global companies that purchase, handle, ship, and process grain, oilseed, and legume crops while paying prices that are often less than the farmer's cost of raising the crops.

Land reform has been a headline issue across the Global South for centuries, but we also need a thoroughgoing version of land reform in the United States. We need not only the buyout and breakup of the largest farms to create more small farms, but also a renewal of rural cultures and economies and their connection to the land. Our once racially diverse farming sector needs to re-diversify. In 1920, there were almost a million Black farmers in America—14 percent of all farmers—owning 15 million acres of land. By 1997, there were fewer than 20,000 Black-owned farms, and they occupied just 2 million acres. The decline was a result of racist bank and governmental lending policies, forced partitioning of landholdings, denial of government benefits to Black families unless they sold their land, and the general decline in profitability of small farms. These factors, as well as the persistence of Jim Crow racism in the South, spurred the twentieth-century movement of 6 million Black people from the rural South to northern cities in what came to be known as the Great Migration.[117]

One precedent for land reform in this country was the New Deal–era buyout and breakup of large Southern plantations in order to establish agricultural communities for former tenant-farming families. The new communities were segregated, and only thirteen of the approximately one hundred farming settlements created were all-Black communities. Furthermore, the Black farmers were often consigned to the least fertile or most flood-prone lands.[118] Each family in the community received a few dozen acres of land, a newly built wood-frame house, and farm outbuildings. The communities established schools and health care facilities, and set up cooperative stores and cotton gins. Despite racial discrimination, many of the Black communities thrived for decades, even after conservatives in Congress dismantled Farm Services in the 1940s.[119]

The Federation of Southern Cooperatives was formed in 1967 to organize and serve Black farmers' cooperatives and credit unions. As of 2018, the federation encompassed more than seventy co-ops and other Black farm groups, with a total membership of more than 20,000 families. More broadly, the dramatic twentieth-century decline in numbers of Black farms and farmers has reversed. In the single decade from 2002 to 2012, the number of Black U.S. farm operators rose 28 percent.[120] Today, there are grassroots groups such as the National Black Farmers

Association and the Southeastern African American Farmers' Organic Network working to build a new, far-flung network of Black farms and farming communities. Soul Fire Farm and the Northeast Farmers of Color Alliance have joined forces to publish a guide for farmers and communities titled "Action Steps for Food Sovereignty." The latter two organizations make land available to farmers and land stewards, help communities with funding to establish land- and food-based enterprises, and provide training for new farmers. Soul Fire publishes a "reparations map" of dozens of Black and Indigenous farms across North America, encouraging support for them.[121] Soul Fire Farm cofounder Leah Penniman said in a 2019 interview:

> I think it's really important for us to remember that the
> land is not a commodity or just a material entity. Again
> harkening back to Afro-Indigenous cosmology, the land is a
> living, breathing, sovereign being. I have spiritual mentors in
> Ghana, West Africa, called the Queen Mothers, or manye,
> and they were really incredulous to learn that farmers in
> the United States would plant a seed and they wouldn't
> pray over it, or dance, or offer any libation, and they
> expected that seed to grow and produce nourishing food
> for the community. And they were like, "That's why your
> society is sick, clearly, because you're just seeing this as a
> transactional relationship with the earth—input, output."…
> So when we talk about land sovereignty, or farming, or any
> of this stuff, we have to remember to really pay attention to
> the needs of the earth. Industrial agriculture is destroying
> the planet, is a major driver of climate change, of land use
> conversions and water withdrawals. We know how to do an
> agriculture that's different, that can feed the planet without

destroying the resource base. And we both need to do that in a material sense, through those actions, and also to consider the earth as living.[122]

If we're to have land reform in North America, a central element must be recognition of Indigenous sovereignty. Dina Gilio-Whitaker, the author of *As Long as Grass Grows: The Indigenous Fight for Environmental Justice, from Colonization to Standing Rock*, told the website *Earther* in 2019:

> The way sovereignty is understood, to whatever degree it's understood in the popular discourse, is about governance, self-determination. The world is organized into countries, but they are really organized as states, and this implies a strictly political understanding of things. But for Native people, sovereignty is deeply connected to land....For us, when we talk about sovereignty, we're talking about protecting our reservation boundaries, for sure. But it's also about getting land back. Considering that 48 percent of all the land in the Western United States is public lands, you can give some land back."[123]

Land reform must incorporate labor rights as well. As a first step toward ending the exploitation of migrant farmworkers, for example, it has been proposed that a path to citizenship be made available to them, because they are in the most essential of occupations. But change must go deeper. Just as most plantations of the South were broken up, the big commercial produce farms of today should be divided into smaller family farms, to be owned and operated by those who labor for wages on those lands today. The idea is not purely hypothetical. Immigrant farmworkers across the country have been striking out on their own and starting new farms for years. The number of Latino-owned farms in the

United States has grown by over 35 percent since 2000, to more than 67,000. A large share of the owner-operators are former migrant farmworkers, and many are from farming backgrounds in Mexico or Central America. They typically grow a diverse array of crops, mostly fresh produce, and often using sustainable or organic methods.[124] However, the proportion of Latino farmers benefiting from federal conservation programs or receiving other government payments is only one-fourth to one-half as large as the proportion of white farmers who receive such payments.[125] In interviewing seventy immigrant farmers in Washington State, Minnesota, California, Virginia, and New York, Laura-Anne Minkoff-Zern of Syracuse University concluded:

> Their farming practices do not fit within a purely industrial mode of production, and their farming choices are not the most profitable. Despite their mode of farming fitting within the framework of alternative production, which generally garners a higher selling price, they are not getting the same increased share of the dollar from the organic and local farming movement compared to White farmers. In my observations at farmers' markets in all these regions, immigrant farmers of color generally sold at lower prices and were less likely to be certified organic (and therefore less able to charge price premiums associated with organic certification). Many immigrant farmers struggle to enter markets in higher-paying neighborhoods, due to a sense of exclusion and a well-connected community of White farmers, which is largely inaccessible to them.[126]

Although the farmers she interviewed often earned no more income than they had earned as wage laborers on the big commercial farms, Minkoff-Zern found that "many immigrant farmers possess a wealth of knowledge regarding alternative farming practices and choose to continue them as it fulfills a desire to return to a land-based way of life, reflecting their former livelihoods."

REDUCING EMISSIONS FROM FOOD PRODUCTION

THE ANCESTORS OF the Gullah/Geechee Nation were captured by slavers in West Africa and brought to coastal South Carolina and Georgia. Freed after the Civil War, the Gullah/Geechee Nation remained on the region's sea islands and has continued farming, fishing, and oystering, while riding out at least 150 hurricanes since the 1850s. Chief Queen Quet wrote in 2019 that her community "has been self-sufficient and resilient in this area since the 1600s," but is currently "not only dealing with issues of economic inequity, but also environmental injustice which has and continues to cause displacement of Gullah/Geechee from the southeastern coast. For those that remain there, they are literally on the front shoreline of climate change and sea level rise."[127] Since the 1950s, they have lost much of their land, as well as the integrity of their seashore, to vacation-home and tourism development, but they have continued to sustain themselves and their culture. That includes the catching of shrimp and harvesting of oysters using traditional methods. Ricky Wright, vice president of the Gullah/Geechee Fishing Association, told CNN, "I fished with my father ever since I've been seven or eight. It passes down because it's just a natural thing for us—my parents did it, I'm quite sure my parents' parents did it, and it just descended down."[128]

The community has a long, proven record of mitigating the impacts of climate change while maintaining food security. According to the climate justice website *Grist*, "The Gullah/Geechee Nation has a number of methods that cities can adopt as they plan for climate adaptation. One major project on that front involves helping restore oyster reef and beds along the Carolina shoreline as a foundation for replenishing maritime forest, which helps kneecap oncoming storms from the Atlantic. The oyster habitat helps protect adjacent shorelines from erosion."[129] All is not well, however: "The Gullah/Geechee fishers and farmers once thrived by protecting these habitats, making sure they weren't overfished or destroyed by development, but the seafood and vacation markets have overpowered them in recent decades." Rapid warming of the Southeast's coastal waters has depleted the shrimp and oyster beds, and saltwater is intruding inland.[130] Queen Quet says that, seeing these impacts, her community has been raising alarms about climate change for the past twenty years, so far to no avail.

From the Carolina coast to California's Central Valley, food production not only continues to be undermined by greenhouse warming, but in its industrial mode is also generating copious quantities of greenhouse gases. Only by following the example of Indigenous communities and working with the Earth, rather than fighting it, can agriculture reduce its climate impact. Wes Jackson and Robert Jensen write:

No farmer has ever gone out to the barn to start the day and discovered that a baby tractor had been born overnight. For farmers who work with horses, the birth of a foal would not be surprising. That observation may seem silly, but it highlights an important contrast: Machines cannot reproduce or maintain themselves. Creatures can. The tractor comes out of the industrial mind, while the horse is creaturely. The tractor is the product of an energy-intensive human-designed system, while the horse is the product of an information-intensive biological process that emerges from earth and sun. The implications of this difference are rarely acknowledged in the dominant culture, but we believe they are crucial to explore, now more than ever.[131]

Pre-industrial farming produced quantities of food containing about ten calories worth of chemical energy for each calorie of energy expended (mostly by humans and animals) to produce them. Today, mechanized, high-input agriculture produces higher yields per acre; however, it produces not ten but only one calorie or less of food energy for each calorie expended in production. Most energy input is in the form of fossil fuels for running machinery and manufacturing fertilizer. Neither industrial farming nor manufacturing the complex array of industrial hardware used in today's mode of agriculture is currently possible without burning large volumes of fossil fuel and contaminating the biosphere with countless tons of greenhouse emissions. Tractors indeed do not reproduce.

Most of the tillage, sowing, fertilization, spraying, irrigation, and harvesting being done on America's 300 million–plus acres of field crops is powered by diesel or other liquid fuels. The horsepower that can be generated by a diesel-fired engine will not easily be replicated without fossil fuels. Using actual horses or other draft animals to provide all of the horsepower needed nationwide would require growing an impossible number of acres of feed grains. Biodiesel made from oilseed crops like soybeans is sometimes blended in small proportion with petroleum diesel for on-farm use; however, options for completely eliminating diesel and other fossil fuels from field crop production are limited. Tractors can be built or modified to run on 100 percent biodiesel, but that does not eliminate their ecological impact. That's because replacing all diesel with biodiesel in today's agriculture would require a massive expansion of cropland to grow those oilseeds for use in biodiesel. That would extend cultivation into vast new landscapes, compounding the negative ecological impacts of farming any annual crop: soil erosion, chemical contamination of groundwater and streams, greenhouse emissions, and threats to biodiversity. A better approach could be biogas produced by bacterial digestion of food wastes, leftover farm biomass such as straw and stalks, and manure from livestock. The biogas, mostly methane, could be used to fuel tractors or combine harvesters, while the carbon dioxide that's produced during digestion of the wastes is captured and kept out of the atmosphere. The solids left behind can be returned to the soil as a rich source of plant nutrients and organic matter (and without the emissions of greenhouse gases like methane and nitrous oxide that result from applying raw wastes to the field). Major manufacturers have produced biogas-burning versions of their standard tractors. Biogas from waste has the advantage of not requiring additional land acreage for expansion of grain or oilseed production; however, the amount of gas that can be produced is limited by the quantities of food, crop, and animal wastes available.

Why not go full-tech, using electric tractors and combines that are charged by wind or solar power? There are cottage industries and startups producing small electric-powered tractors for garden use or for industrial use on hard surfaces. Pulling heavy implements with a large electric tractor across a crumbly soil surface, however, would require an enormous, very high-voltage battery. Likewise for a combine harvester, which needs energy to run its reaping and threshing mechanisms as well as the drive train. In both cases, the battery would also need a very high capacity, to run the tractor or combine for a full day between charges. Some showy publicity from the big manufacturers notwithstanding, electrification of farming is not anticipated anytime soon.[132]

Aside from traction, the biggest use of fossil fuel in agriculture is the industrial production of nitrogen fertilizer, which involves the combustion of huge amounts of natural gas. The expansion of other methods to get nitrogen into the soil in a form usable by plants, and in the large quantities necessary, is required. The chief such method will be the longstanding practice of growing legume crops, which, with the help of bacteria, take nitrogen gas from the air and fix it in compounds that plants can metabolize. Such crops, which include beans and peas of all kinds and forages such as alfalfa and clover, are already grown on large scale around the world. If their acreage expands further to provide soil nitrogen in crop rotations, less acreage will be available for other crops. And that will be just fine, because the most effective action we can take to reduce energy use and greenhouse emissions in farming is simply to stop trying to produce so much.

There is plenty of room for cutting back on crop production. Output from U.S. agriculture amounts to about 4,000 calories per day per person—twice as much energy as the average person needs to ingest daily in food form. Looking for the best opportunities for cutting energy use most quickly without causing food shortages, energy analysts publishing in the journal *Nature Sustainability* landed on what they saw as the two best prospects: elimination of fuel ethanol and tight restriction of meat production.

The bulk of the biofuel produced today is grain ethanol intended to substitute for gasoline in passenger vehicles. This is a total waste, because the production of fuel ethanol, from the corn field to the gas pump, requires as much energy in the form of fossil fuels as the final product provides to the vehicle's engine. In the end, no energy or emissions are saved. But while biofuel production barely breaks even, energetically speaking, meat production does much worse. To produce one calorie of meat biomass, the industry on average uses about three calories from grains and seven more calories from plant vegetation such as pasture. Eliminating confined feeding facilities and growing food crops on just a portion of the acreage currently sown to corn, soybean, and other feed grains for livestock, as discussed earlier, would provide ample nutrition for Americans with vastly lower energy use and emissions.

The authors of the *Nature Sustainability* paper concluded that "reducing meat and liquid biofuel consumption offers a remarkably clear improvement to energy consumption and upstream resources, particularly land and water use. Obviously, we recognize the enormity of the socioeconomic, behavioral, and nutritional complexities and challenges associated with these paths forward. But we also contend that a sustainable future without substantive reductions in energy consumption is not possible."[133]

The conversion of field-crop production away from fossil fuels will not consist of a simple switch to a single alternative energy source. It will involve some biogas, some biodiesel, maybe some hydrocarbons from wind power, even a lot of horses and oxen, and, for a long time to come, diesel fuel. While the elimination of fossil fuels from road transportation is imperative and will require a deep reduction in the use of vehicles, food production is essential. In a world where we manage to end the climate emergency, agriculture may be the last activity in which we continue to use fossil fuels.

"ANTICIPATE COMPLEX, UNCERTAIN AND CHAOTIC CONDITIONS AS TYPICAL"

ACTION ON A broad front can temper the ecological and atmospheric damage, worker exploitation, nutritional degradation, and other problems that arise from food production and processing as they are now practiced. But agriculture will never become genuinely humane and ecologically sustainable until we deal with the literal roots of the problem. The current fragility of the North American food system has its origins in European settlers' theft of the continent's forest and prairie landscapes, the killing and purging of Indigenous people who lived there, and the clear-cutting and plowing of those lands in order to kill their diverse, perennial native vegetation and replace it with shallow-rooted monocultures of annual European crops. For decades, crop production on many of those depleted landscapes was wholly dependent on the labor of enslaved African people, and later, on the cruelty of sharecropping. Eventually, most Black farm families lost their claim to the land altogether. The plowing continued, destroying soil ecosystems that had depended on the continuous presence of living roots. Production of annual crops in soils depleted of organic matter, mineral nutrients, and microbial life has now, for more than a century, required heavy inputs of synthetic fertilizers and toxic chemicals, and destruction of biodiversity. This is variously referred to as replacing soil with oil, or maintaining crops in intensive-care units. We can find partial short-term answers for the human and ecological damage that agriculture has wrought on America, but in the long term, we need a transformation of rural society toward diversity and justice, and a displacement of annual monoculture cropping by multi-species, perennial landscapes that can produce ample food while at least partially restoring soil ecosystems to the state of health they enjoyed under the long-gone prairies and forests and the care of the Indigenous people who lived there.

The annual grain crops that supply, directly and indirectly, the bulk of our diet are incapable of maintaining the rich belowground ecosystems of organic matter and nutrients—webs of fungi, bacteria, nematodes, earthworms, insects, small animals—that thrive in soils nurtured by the roots of diverse stands of perennial plants. Ninety-five percent of the vegetation that covered pre-agricultural landscapes consisted of diverse, perennial plant communities. Those natural landscapes never suffered from soil erosion or degradation. They supported prolific biodiversity both above and below the soil surface. They did not pollute streams or groundwater. They stored carbon from the atmosphere. Those perennial ecosystems were stripped away and replaced by crops that are regrown from seed at the start of every season and whose roots die at season's end. The

result has been soil erosion, depletion of soil nutrients, water pollution, loss of soil carbon into the atmosphere, and catastrophic biodiversity loss—mass extinctions. In America's rural regions, we have
seen a parallel loss of cultural health and diversity.

Grain farmers have scrambled heroically over the centuries to
mitigate the damage they inherited, but as long as they have no
choice but to grow annual crops, restoring agricultural ecosystems
to health will be impossible. In recent years, efforts to address the
problem by domesticating and breeding perennial grain-producing
crops have progressed from local beginnings at the Land Institute in
the U.S. central plains to be taken up by nationwide and worldwide
research networks. The process will take time, but results are starting to emerge. Highly productive perennial rice varieties are being
grown on tens of thousands of acres in southwest China. A perennial
cousin of wheat known as Kernza is under pilot production in the
U.S. plains and upper Midwest. Breeding work is continuing with
those and other new crops under development.[134]

In the long run, it is essential that agriculture go perennial worldwide, but that alone will not engender food systems that sustain both
thriving ecosystems and healthy, just societies. To achieve such complete food systems, researchers Aubrey Streit Krug and Omar Imseeh
Tesdell have called for a "social perennial vision" based on principles of sufficiency, responsibility, and co-creativity. By the authors'
definitions, sufficiency requires us "to reflectively grapple with the
limited powers of people...to shape change, for worse and for better,
and decide what is enough to be satisfied"; responsibility means that
"all humans need to give their time and bodies and attention to the
moral support and needs of all other humans as well as non-human
creatures and the places and processes of the ecosphere"; and co-
creativity is the situation in which "people seek to learn together
with the land rather than destroy a landscape in order to try and
improve it."[135] Here in the United States, we need land reform that
breaks the largely white lock on ownership of the countryside, that

ends to farmworker and food-worker exploitation, and that guarantees sufficient good food for all.

We need greater human diversity in farming both now and in Streit-Krug and Tesdell's "social-perennial vision" for the future.[136] A small step was taken with Congressional passage of the $1.9 trillion Covid relief bill in 2021. It contained $5 billion for farmers of color, intended for debt relief and direct funds, as well as help for farmers and aspiring farmers in acquiring land. But even some who welcomed the bill's farmer assistance provision pointed out that it was a drop in the bucket compared with Black farm families' total estimated losses of $250 to $350 billion over the past century due to racist agricultural policies and appropriation of land by white farmers and developers. Tracy Lloyd McCurty, executive director of the Black Belt Justice Center, made this point eloquently yet diplomatically: "Once again, Black farmers, because of their dedication to organizing, have created liberation for farmers of color. Our farmers are due a field of flowers, not a bouquet, for the sorrow they've carried."[137]

The long struggles carried out by farmers of color can inspire much more sweeping action. In studying the history of Black farmers' cooperatives from the nineteenth century until now, Leah Penniman writes:

> Here was an entire history, blooming into our present, in which Black people's expertise and love of the land and one another was evident. When we as Black people are bombarded with messages that our only place of belonging on land is as slaves, performing dangerous and backbreaking menial labor, to learn of our true and noble history as farmers and ecological stewards is deeply healing.[138]

We also cannot ignore for a moment longer the hundreds of millions of people here and around the world who were regularly going hungry before 2020, or the countless more families who were thrown into hunger by the pandemic's disruption of local and world economies, or the even larger numbers who will join them because of heat- and drought-related crop losses expected as the climate emergency intensifies.

If the United States wants to support the efforts of people of the Global South to get through that greenhouse future, we should start by immediately ceasing all the things we are now doing to degrade living conditions worldwide. As an obvious example, the U.S. government can help limit climate-induced hunger by putting in place mechanisms to speedily eliminate this country's greenhouse emissions and to begin entering into fossil-fuel nonproliferation agreements that can coalesce into a global treaty. If, however, we attempt to construct a wind- and solar-powered society that replicates today's high-energy living arrangements and transportation systems, the result will be the creation of what are being called "green sacrifice zones" in nations that have large deposits of cobalt, lithium, and other metals that go into the batteries and mechanisms essential to renewable electricity systems.[139] Overhauling our economy so that it can function well with far less energy input, along with strict regulation of how and where our energy industry obtains those resources, will be crucial to preventing so-called "green colonialism."

The work of the development sociologist and writer Max Ajl highlights a broad variety of land-based climate actions being carried out every day across the Global South, without help from the North—not high technology but rather, as he puts it, "'low-tech' fixes for crises of climate and underdevelopment, fixes which bloom like wildflowers the world over." They include hundreds of millions of farmers associated with the worldwide peasant movement La Via Campesina, practicing agroecology; farmers converting to agroforestry to stop soil erosion and carbon loss; pastoralists following climate-friendly grazing techniques; and Indigenous people on every continent who stand as the only barrier between healthy landscapes and plunder by global capitalism. Affluent nations must augment those efforts by providing funds for development and climate mitigation and adaptation, argues Ajl, not under the label of "aid" but in the form of installment payments on the climate reparations we owe the majority of the world's people.[140]

As for the disruption of food economies of the Global South by future disease outbreaks and climatic disasters, our country should push for international agreements declaring that access to sufficient food is an unconditional right, and that in fulfilling that right the desires of private economic interests will have no standing. Policies to fulfill the right to food must protect and support farm families and ensure all households' access to food, but even more is needed. Amartya Sen and Jean Drèze, world experts on this subject, write, "A person's capability to avoid undernourishment may not depend merely on his or her intake of food, but also on the person's access to health care, medical facilities, elementary education, drinking water, and sanitary facilities. Similarly, the prevalence of epidemics and disease in a particular region may also be a factor influencing the extent of undernutrition."[141] To state the obvious, unless these basic elements of a decent standard of living are also guaranteed and pursued independent of business interests, and unless ecological integrity and health can be maintained, the right to food won't be assured.

As the pandemic was building toward its fall peak, Potawatomi author Robin Wall Kimmerer provided this sage advice on ecological limits—an antidote to the vague yearning to "get back to normal":

In the springtime, we were closing down and staying in our homes at the same time as the birds' lives were burgeoning around us. As the pandemic came upon us, we began asking: Where am I going to get food? How are we going to go to the grocery store? Will my family be OK? Where can I go to be safe? I thought, Dang, birds face that same kind of vulnerability every single day. *Where is my food going*

to come from, because you people cut down the last place
I know to get those berries? I'm worried that if I go out, I
could die. Will my family be OK? That's what it's like to be
a bluebird. The medicine we need comes with that ecological compassion. If we can see that the vulnerability we feel
is the very vulnerability that we inflict on the natural world
by our actions, then it's worth it.[142]

In their *Futures* article on the need to radically adjust our expectations for an ecological transition, the group of Australian authors
whom I quoted in Chapter 2 explain:

The nature of the envisaged transition means that we are
entering entirely unexplored territory, and the pathways
that we walk into existence are subject to inherent, irreduc-
ible uncertainty. It is impossible to know up front just how
these pathways will unfold, the full range of challenges
that will be encountered along the way, and where the
novel responses to them will take us. As such, there is very
good reason to think that the situations that emerge will be
very different from the expectations created by any model
constructed or plan conceived today. It seems prudent to
conclude that global-scale transition away from fossil fuels
leads humanity into the post-normal realm of "unthought
futures." Here actors will do better to anticipate complex,
uncertain and chaotic conditions as typical, rather than
extreme outliers.[143]

Writing weeks before the Covid-19 pandemic struck, they argued
presciently that plans for creating climate-safe societies that function
just like today's societies—that is, plans for getting back to business

as usual—have so far been rooted in a belief that surprise developments are deviations from a natural state of order and equilibrium, a world that can be restored through "orthodox governance institutions." Unfortunately, they concluded, "the analysis presented here implies that this stance is no longer tenable." The time for orthodox governance has long passed. Uprooting such orthodoxy won't be easy, but clearing a path to a livable future now depends on it.

4.

PEOPLE HAVE THE POWER

We assume that unity can be created without doing really difficult work together. Instead, we need to center unity around issues that we deeply care about. Unity should come from similar visions of the future rather than only the virtue of one's identity.

—Angela Davis, March 2021

ABOLISH SYSTEMIC RACISM and state-sanctioned killing. Ensure safety, well-being, and justice for historically marginalized communities, families, and people. Free society of fossil fuels, air and water contamination, and greenhouse warming. Guarantee access to goods and services for all households regardless of occupations or incomes. Build a robust, ecologically sound, inclusive, and just food system to replace today's fragile, destructive, cruel system. Create a new health system that serves everyone. And get it done together, with all sectors of society at the table.

That's quite a to-do list, and it's just the start of what's required of us. It would be daunting enough even had we not painted ourselves into a technological corner, and even if the most politically and economically powerful forces in the country were not determined to keep the system the way it is. Just getting started requires unprecedented solidarity, optimism, and mobilization. As Adrian Parr says in her pre-pandemic book *The Wrath of Capital: Neoliberalism and Climate Change*, "Habitual thinking and praxis have to be replaced by a more utopian imagination"—one that inspires people to resist and replace the current system before it's too late.

ROUGH TERRAIN AHEAD

LONGSTANDING ANTI-VACCINE PROPAGANDA has merged with a stubborn subculture of individualistic resistance to public-health measures, raising the risk that we will be living with an ominously evolving Covid-19 virus well into the future.[144] And once we finally do achieve long-term suppression, we will still face the possibility that this and the two other deadly coronaviruses that emerged between 2002 and 2020 are, in scientists' words, the tip of a very large iceberg. Until we stop and reverse the ecological encroachment and damage that trigger both medical and environmental disasters, we could find ourselves dealing with both simultaneously—and more—for a long time to come. Complications will result. Creating a just society that runs on less industrially produced energy will require a wholesale movement toward public transit and away from the private vehicles that have provided a refuge from viral spread. A move toward multi-unit housing such as apartment buildings, as opposed to large single-family houses, will be highly effective in reducing energy use and greenhouse emissions but could increase the risk of exposure. Facing a long-term need to prevent spread of future diseases for which human bodies have limited defenses, will we have the long-range vision and social solidarity required to make sweeping changes, redefine "normal," and create the foundation for us to collectively restore the planet's—and our own—health?

Humanity's past greenhouse emissions could be even more troublesome than pandemic pathogens in complicating efforts to reduce future emissions to zero. In the decades during which Puerto Rico will be working on its new, resilient, renewable energy infrastructure, for example, greenhouse warming will continue and, among other things, further supercharge hurricanes. What if the electric grid were challenged every few years by storms of Maria's intensity or worse? Can a territory cut its own greenhouse emissions and become more resilient to disasters while at the same time repeatedly building back from disasters caused by the world's past failure to curb emissions? Consider the proposal to install interconnected solar microgrids serving ten households each throughout the Puerto Rico. Maria inflicted serious harm on solar and wind farms in several locations, and future storms could do so again. In the widespread rooftop solar generation envisioned as a part of microgrid systems, not only the equipment but also the roofs themselves will need to withstand winds at least as strong as Maria's. That won't be easy. Puerto Rico's high degree of economic inequality and the related variation in housing quality, from rock-solid to flimsy, meant that countless roofs were destroyed throughout the island. The full number is not known, but it is huge. The U.S. Federal Emergency Management Agency and the U.S. Army together distributed approximately 185,000 tarps for use as temporary roofs, and they were far too few to meet demand.[145] Any ambitious program for rooftop solar installation would have to accompany an even more ambitious upgrade of the island's housing quality, with extra-rigorous code requirements for roofs, whether or not the roofs will be supporting solar arrays. And all families still living in old, storm-vulnerable homes will require safe, affordable housing.

Climate disruption poses other threats to climate mitigation and adaptation. For example, how can a just transition to a low-emissions economy be systematically planned if, due to intolerable heat and humidity in the Sun Belt and Mississippi Valley, wildfires on the West Coast and in the South, constant pummeling by hurricanes on the Gulf Coast, and sea-level rise on all coasts, we become a nation of climate refugees, with the affluent inevitably snapping up the safe ground? And, given the harsh, often cruel U.S. and European treatment of refugees in recent years, what even worse indignities will be endured by even larger waves of people fleeing the floods, droughts, and fires expected as the climate emergency intensifies worldwide?

However daunting the obstacles to ecological transformation that have been created by the damaged ecosphere itself, the strongest force preventing that transformation remains the determination of the rich and powerful to ensure growth of their profits and investment portfolios, along with their reluctance to improve the economic system to more justly share wealth with the millions of people who produce it. We can have ecological sustainability or capital accumulation, but not both. We can have economic sufficiency for all or wealth for the few, but not both. Even if there is massive public spending on new energy infrastructure in the post-pandemic years, a continuation of business as usual will leave the economy as a whole where it is now: under the control of corporations. In the energy sector, the fossil fuel industry and ancillary enterprises—for example, pipeline and equipment manufacturers and private utilities—have deep pockets and great political power. They will resist any moves, however small, toward nationalization or Cap-and-Adapt restrictions on their commercial goals. Indeed, corporations in all sectors of the economy will jump to kill any discussion of a cap. Planned allocation of fuels and electricity to ensure essential production and services—a necessity in a climate-safe future—will create winners and losers among corporations, and "winning" in this context will mean being able to carry on with business, but on an externally constrained energy supply. Such a policy will be unacceptable in the economic power centers.

Almost every news cycle brings word of corporate intentions to become part of the climate solution. Beware of all such pledges, especially when they aim for "net zero" emissions or "carbon neutrality" by some future date. Electric utilities are making some of the more overblown claims in this regard. In a January 2021 report, "The Dirty Truth About Utility Climate Pledges," the Sierra Club deftly punctured the U.S. electric power sector's inflated promises to make meaningful emissions reductions. In it, analysts assigned each company a classroom-style grade of 0 to 100, awarding points for commitments to stop using coal or to build up renewable energy capacity, while subtracting points for planning to build natural gas–fired capacity. Only three out of seventy-nine utilities earned a score of 75 or better, the threshold for taking actions consistent with avoiding more than 1.5 degrees of atmospheric warming. Most were performing much more poorly, whether or not they had made climate pledges. Companies with pledges for "net zero" emissions earned a collective score of only 20, almost as miserable as the overall score of 14 earned by non-pledging companies.[146]

The power sector of the European Union (EU) is following its own questionable path to "net zero" emissions. Energy policy currently requires member countries to generate 20 percent of their electricity from renewable sources. The EU classifies burning of biomass as a renewable process, so over the past decade, biomass, mostly in the form of wood pellets, has come to account for well over half of the union's "renewable" electricity supply. Because the wood comes mostly from live trees, not waste, the result has been extensive deforestation in some Eastern European nations. The *Guardian* reports that "as a result, the Estonian land-use sector, which includes forestry, is expected to switch from being a carbon sink to an emitter of carbon by 2030."[147] Damage being done to forest ecosystems continues to be severe.

Corporations in all sectors of the U.S. economy, not just energy, are making climate pledges based on little more than sleight of hand.

Because the companies see no way to profitably reach bona fide "zero emissions" or survive without energy from fossil fuels, their most common ploy is to "offset" each ton of emissions they produce by paying to fund projects that will either prevent or capture a ton of emissions elsewhere. The projects selling offsets, however, almost never reduce emissions by anything close to the extent claimed.[148] Any of the rare climate-friendly projects that *are* effective should, of course, be funded and pursued on their own merits anyway. Therefore, one can view the sale of "pay to pollute" offsets as canceling out the offset-selling project's successful emissions reduction. Meanwhile, corporations can benefit at both ends of the transaction. Today, agriculture giants are selling credits to big industrial polluters based on unverified claims of capturing huge quantities of atmospheric carbon in the soil. Even more fanciful are plans for vast new energy-hungry industrial sites to capture carbon dioxide directly from the air in order to sell offset credits.[149] Getting to zero emissions is a necessary target. "Net zero" is a mirage.The tightening of resources and production will create a need for additional policies and programs that also are anathema to the corporate sector. Governments will need to provide for job retraining, cut the length of the work week in half so there will be enough jobs to go around, establish not just a minimum wage but a living wage, provide income support where needed, and ensure universal basic services (with food and health care at the top of the list). And all of that, I have been arguing for some time, will require steeply progressive taxes on the income and wealth of the most affluent 33 percent of households, and hikes in corporate taxes.[150]

Having a solid Democratic majority in the national electorate and Democrats in the White House will not be enough to achieve sufficient progress on climate, public health, racial justice, or economic equality. Few national Democratic officeholders will support proposals like Cap and Adapt to directly eliminate oil and natural gas unless they are pushed hard by the electorate. Taking the necessary action on climate will require that the federal government assign higher priority to the Earth and its people than to economic growth. Fear of political attacks by the economic powers that be, plus a deep desire not to be seen as "radical" by their own constituents prevents most Democratic lawmakers from supporting even mildly ambitious proposals like the Green New Deal.

It would be the understatement of all understatements to say that corporate and political resistance to strong action against fossil fuels will be difficult to overcome. Indeed, the necessary change will be impossible without a broad, deep transformation of how Americans understand their relationship to capitalism, the inherent imbalances of power between themselves and the investing and owning classes, and how those imbalances perpetuate disinformation, inaction, and chronic injustice. We need the sort of reawakening that swept across America and into Washington and corporate boardrooms during the Great Depression, petrifying the plutocrats. However, this ground-swell will need to go much broader and deeper than the one that emerged in the New Deal era—and this time around, it must deliver results for all, not just for white Americans. In this, the Black Lives Matter movement is already taking the lead. Patrisse Cullors, one of the movement's founders, told *Politico* in November 2020, "We are both marching and protesting. And we are going to the voting booth. Those are multiple tools in our toolbox to change our system." [151]

This effort will run up against a phenomenon that, while not as formidable as corporate power, will present a dangerous, unpredictable hazard: an obdurate political bloc, comprising perhaps one-third of voters, that is deeply committed to imposing white minority rule throughout this century and beyond. It existed before 2016 but became a potent political force under Trump's Republican Party. It survives Trump's 2020 electoral defeat and will plague us through the very years when transformation of the economy and society will be needed as urgently as at any time since the Civil War. Political scientist Cara Daggett draws direct connections between patriarchy, fossil fuel dependence, and the U.S. drift toward authoritarianism: "Fossil fuel extraction and consumption can function as a performance of masculinity, even as it also serves the interests of fossil capitalism. Similarly, the concept of petro-masculinity emphasizes that global warming may sometimes be interpreted as a breach in the patriarchal dam....Taking petro-masculinity seriously means paying attention to the thwarted desires of privileged patriarchies as they lose their fossil fantasies."[152]

This retrograde, pro-authoritarian, mostly working-class voting bloc—comprising relentless opponents of racial justice, superstition-bound deniers of Earth sciences as well as the germ theory of disease, and believers in their own individual rights over any concept of the public interest—is a political force in just enough states and regions to undermine attempts to transform U.S. society for the common good. Their power depends on gerrymandering, the structure of the Senate and Electoral College, and the support or acquiescence of countless Republican elected officials who channel their energy to support the economic interests of the corporate class, their true masters. This retrograde minority has the proven ability to prevent things that a sane, humane society would do, such as encourage public health, prevent state-sanctioned killing of people based on race, and protect the Earth from overheating caused by human pollution. They have shown their intentions to block any progress toward such goals not only through corruption of the political system but also through mob violence. Political actions must be mounted against this threat throughout the same years in which aggressive action must be taken on climate, health, and justice issues. Compromise with white supremacists and their defenders is unthinkable.

LOCKED IN?

POLITICAL OBSTACLES TO the necessary transformation of society can and must be overcome, but clearing those kinds of hurdles will take us only part of the way. After two centuries, the consequence of settler colonialism in North America has been the creation of a society with fragile physical foundations that would crumble without an extravagant, continuous influx of energy and other resources. Strategies, some better than others, have been proposed for breaking the "lock-in" of fossil fuels. But as formidable a challenge as that lock-breaking presents, suppressing the fuels themselves is not the thorniest issue. The entire physical foundation of U.S. society is dependent on a colossal, uninterrupted supply of industrially supplied energy. Excessive energy consumption is locked in by our society's dependence on cargo hauling, farming equipment, and manufacturing of steel and concrete, all of which are powered via direct burning of fossil fuels and required by excessively large, electricity-hungry houses (those owned by households with incomes over $80,000 and averaging almost 3,000 square feet); by oversize, tightly sealed office blocks, big-box stores, and other commercial spaces that require round-the-clock energy-intensive climate control; by suburban and exurban sprawl fed by the slow crawl of commuter traffic along twelve-lane roads ironically called "expressways"; by the post-pandemic push to ensure that airlines and interstate highways remain the predominant means of long-distance passenger travel, rather than building up passenger rail; and, above all, an economic system that cannot function without overproduction of goods and services. Income and wealth inequality often rule out living patterns that reduce energy consumption. For instance, many people can't afford to live near work or buy super-efficient vehicles and appliances. Many homeowners can't afford top-level insulation or solar energy equipment, while renters don't even have the option to install them.

Much is made of the seemingly small per-capita ecological footprint of large, densely populated cities, where public transportation, neighborhood businesses, and small living quarters in multistory buildings are the rule, and where everybody walks. In their call for "radical urbanization," the so-called ecomodernists would herd everyone into huge, high-tech cities connected by high-speed rail lines running through a countryside devoid of humans.[153] While accurate in some particulars, the "dense living equals green living" formula is, overall, a myth. First, it's important to note that the pleasant "green" big-city lifestyle is beyond economic reach for the majority of America's urban-dwellers. Second, it's not green—not necessarily worse than other affluent ways of life, but also not ecologically sustainable. City-dwellers may think they have escaped the lock-in of high resource consumption, but the supply lines that make today's seemingly climate-friendly urban way of life possible are many and long. The oil and gas fields, mines, manufacturing plants, warehouses, and freight lines that supply U.S. metropolises are in the distant counties, states, or countries to whose climate accounts the excess greenhouse emissions are charged and whose residents have a lower, heavily polluted quality of life while facing lock-ins of their own. Consider people who grow our staple field crops, who live by necessity in sparsely populated areas, often where the nearest grocery store may be fifty miles away and the carbon footprint is accordingly high.

Thanks to the lock-ins imposed by technology and living patterns, the United States consumes about twice as much total energy per capita as the average European country, and four times as much as some countries with good living standards, while still failing to guarantee all people adequate food and health care, freedom from environmental degradation, or protection from state-sanctioned violence.[154] Freeing ourselves from fuels and technologies that abuse the Earth is entirely possible, but it will require wholesale changes in infrastructure and living arrangements—changes on a massive scale.

We tend to avoid discussing the full extent to which our species has already damaged the Earth, and how much more damage is to come, for fear of inducing a sense of collective futility and despair. However, research shows that optimistic messages of progress in curbing climate change do not, as hoped, spur people to engage in more vigorous climate action. On the contrary, it is messages focusing on the growing threat posed by greenhouse warming that create strong motivation for action.[155] In other words, a clear-eyed discussion of past and future damage—one that emphasizes that in trying to limit future damage, we are not helpless—can galvanize, and if there's one thing humanity needs as we face the 2020s, it's galvanization. In that spirit, I will quote here at length from *Uncivilisation: The Dark Mountain Manifesto*, which was unveiled in 2009 as the founding document of the Dark Mountain Project, a virtual gathering place and publisher for writers and artists who acknowledge that we live in the "age of ecocide":

> After a quarter century of complacency, in which we were invited to believe in bubbles that would never burst, prices that would never fall, the end of history...a familiar human story is being played out. It is the story of an empire corroding from within. It is the story of a people who believed, for a long time, that their actions did not have consequences. It is the story of how that people will cope with the crumbling of their own myth....

> We are, we tell ourselves, the only species ever to have attacked nature and won. In this, our unique glory is contained....The bubble is that delusion of isolation under which we have labored for so long. The bubble has cut us off from life on the only planet we have, or are ever likely to have. The bubble is civilization. Consider the structures on which that bubble has been built. Its foundations are geological: coal, oil, gas – millions upon millions of years of ancient sunlight, dragged from the depths of the planet and burned with abandon....

We are the first generations born into a new and unprecedented age—the age of ecocide. To name it thus is not to presume the outcome, but simply to describe a process which is underway. The ground, the sea, the air, the elemental backdrops to our existence—all these our economics has taken for granted, to be used as a bottomless [trash dump], endlessly able to dilute and disperse the tailings of our extraction, production, consumption....

Today, humanity is up to its neck in denial about what it has built, what it has become—and what it is in for. Ecological and economic collapse unfold before us and, if we acknowledge them at all, we act as if this were a temporary problem, a technical glitch. Centuries of hubris block our ears like wax plugs; we cannot hear the message which reality is screaming at us.[156]

Is it possible to fully absorb the message reality is screaming at us and not find ourselves paralyzed by a feeling of helplessness? Yes, it is; we know this because there are lots of individuals and groups—including the Dark Mountain Project itself—who are placing their bets on the possibility that all is not lost, and are working tirelessly to help pull us back from the brink and onto the path toward a just and livable future. Let us now turn to them.

KEYS TO THE LOCK-IN?

In 2019, the economist Timothée Parrique completed his 872-page doctoral dissertation, titled "The Political Economy of Degrowth."[157] Built on foundations laid by degrowth researchers such as Giorgos Kallis, Jason Hickel, Julia Steinberger, and Riccardo

Mastini,[158] this masterwork includes a third and final section that provides a bracing antidote for despair, a glimpse of a practical path leading away from the brink. In summing up his conclusions, Parrique listed a number of items that should serve as both principles and goals in any effort to create a society that operates within sufficiently strict ecological limits.

Parrique's framework includes a list of long-familiar principles, including local stewardship of ecosystems and resource sovereignty, sustainability, elimination of waste, and localized production and consumption. It is based largely on the transformation of not only what we produce but why, how, and how much we work, on the grounds that "the issue of work is not only about employment and production, but more fundamentally about how we perceive time and what this entails for social-ecological justice." For a society to function well within ecological limits will require "placing limits on both income and wealth" and pursuing "democratic ownership of business [and] promotion of small, not-for-profit, cooperatives." The world of labor must be transformed, to ensure "decent work, both in its content (what is being produced and why) and in its form (how is it being produced and by whom)." All of this will require that society "challenge the centrality of market-coordinated, commodity-producing, paid employment in social life and construct a less work-centered society."

In Parrique's vision for transformation, "what is not needed should not be made," and what is made should be for "planet and people, not profit." We must treat technology "as a tool, not a master." We must value "communities instead of commodities" and "less stuff, more relationships," while ensuring "sufficiency for all, excess for none."[159] In the transformed society, "sovereign banking reclaims money as a public utility [and] the creation and destruction of money should be organized democratically following social and ecological criteria."

In his attempts to interconnect all of this into a "coherent transition strategy," Parrique writes that he arrived at an encouraging insight: "Operationalizing degrowth is not as fanciful as its detractors would think. In fact, I came back from this journey with one powerful sentiment: Degrowth is within reach. All the policies required to get a degrowth transition started are available today. There is little to lose and a lot to win, and the only thing still lacking is our own collective self-confidence in our ability to build an alternative, more desirable future." Noting that in today's world, "policies are being crafted every day," he concludes:

> The conundrum is therefore the following: participate in policymaking while giving up revolutionary ideals or stay true to such ideas and refuse to partake in the discussion. I think that choice should be refused in favor of a third option: to engage in policymaking with the goal of introducing revolutionary reforms. Both tactics and strategy are important. Tactics are the everyday battles, the opportunities of the moment. In the same way, one should not wait for a perfect "degrowth moment" before partaking in policy discussions; instead, one should always be present and work to build our way towards such an opportunity.

"A little to lose and a lot to win"—that's a conclusion that can open doors to action. In the United States, one stubborn obstacle to action has been our culture of individualism, which came into the sharpest relief yet in 2020 with Covid. But this is where we may also begin to see bright spots. The increasingly militant insistence on personal "liberty" above all other values carried out by mask-haters, MAGA rally–goers, and the "tough" guys in the pro-Trump parades of jumbo pickup trucks in 2020 tarnished the reputation of individualism. Meanwhile, a solid majority of Americans have come to support an array of policies such as universal health care, a green transformation, racial justice, and workers' rights, all of which Republicans decry as "socialist." In April 2019, Gallup pollsters asked: "Would some form of socialism be a good thing or a bad thing for the country as a whole?" Forty-three percent of all respondents said it would be a good thing, as did 57 percent of "nonwhite" respondents, 58 percent of those between 18 and 34, and a whopping 70 percent of Democrats.[160] And that poll was taken before the pandemic had pushed into the headlines issues such as inequality, workers' rights, and the role of government. Even as those on the right attacked the word "socialism" throughout the 2020 election season, they were ignored by a majority of voters who were busy embracing policies that would be routine elements of any socialist society.

In her March 2021 op-ed in the *New York Times*, writer Rachel Cohen pointed out that many government policies put in place around the country during the pandemic before 2020 "would have been seen by most people—not to mention most politicians—as radical and politically naïve." There were policies that banned utility shutoffs, imposed eviction moratoria, provided homeless people with independent living spaces (Austin, Texas, went so far as to buy up hotels for that purpose), expanded unemployment benefits, made internet access more available, turned city streets into Covid-safe pedestrian walkways, and approved early releases of incarcerated people. Regarding the last point, a public defender in Virginia told Cohen, "I hope I am able to look a judge in the face when this is over and say, in 2020 you wouldn't have incarcerated this guy, so why are we doing this now?"[161]

With most of the progressive Covid-era policies only temporary, Cohen saw further mass action as necessary to make them permanent and then extend them—for example, by moving on from banning eviction and providing hotel rooms to expanding tenant rights and public housing availability, as well as universal housing vouchers. "It is essential," she wrote, that "we get the word out on what has been accomplished as a result of this crisis and what our government still can do, and to remember what grassroots activists understand deeply: Whether anything happens at all is largely up to us."

If the awakening to racial justice and economic equality now in progress among the U.S. majority can merge with growing awareness that we are careening toward an ecological cliff, there is at least the possibility of a groundswell of support for nationalization and a planned phase-out of fossil fuels, along with a radical redistribution of economic power that will overwhelm the resistance of the plutocrats and the far right. Here and abroad, we have seen ever-escalating challenges to their power: Indigenous uprisings for water protection and against fossil-fuel industries, Extinction Rebellion, the Sunrise Movement, School Climate Strikes, Black Lives Matter, and anti-fascism mobilizations.

Stabilizing the environment and preventing escalating climate catastrophes now requires not just a continuation but an acceleration and merging of the past few years' mobilizations. Democrats in Washington have never voted on, much less passed, legislation strong enough to put an end to greenhouse emissions, or to guarantee universal single-payer health care, or to make police shootings of unarmed people, Black or otherwise, a federal crime. Instead, they have routinely taken voters of color for granted. Democrats have yet to propose slashing the military budget or guaranteeing universal basic services. We must show them that they are mandated to represent the people, not the Silicon Valley tycoons, the natural gas extractors, the pharmaceutical companies, or the police unions.

The widespread, sustained uprising under the banner of Black Lives Matter may best exemplify what is needed in the years ahead. Thousands of marches and rallies took place in 2020 and continue to this day, not only in all major U.S. cities but also in small towns from coast to coast, and in countless places around the world. Many marchers braved assault and arrest by local, state, and federal police. Incensed by police violence against unarmed Black people, a massive and racially diverse cross section of the country mobilized to demand an end to white supremacy and racial injustice in all their forms. Given the open racism that persists in contemporary Republican politics in general and local law enforcement in particular, the Black Lives Matter movement has had ample evidence for the urgency of its demands. In giving those demands voice through protest and organizing, the movement not only has carried national consciousness into a new realm, but always aims to do so in ways that are intersectional, demanding that, in the words of Black Lives Matter cofounder Alicia Garza, "we do better by one another so that we can be more powerful together." "First," Garza writes, "by looking at the world through a lens that is different from that of just white people, we can see how power is distributed unevenly and on what basis, and second, we need to ensure that the world that we fight for, the claim we lay to the future, is one that meets the needs of all who have been marginalized."[162] The path to a livable future depends on our ability to wage multiple struggles at once, and to do so in ways, as Garza describes, that end marginalization.

Ample evidence exists that cessation of ecological destabilization will vastly decrease marginalization, for climate change impacts those with the least resources most. It will take intense public pressure—not just in the voting booth but in the streets—to demand that the political system forge policies that free us from fossil fuels, structural racism, and a capitalist economic system that puts private profit ahead of public health. "Generations of conflict at home and abroad have shaped the environment we live in now," writes Garza. "It is up to us to decide what we will do about how our environment has been shaped and how we have been shaped along with it."[163]

MUTUAL AID

IN THE TENSE, tumultuous period between now and the time when we finally win the deep change we need and deserve, movements for sweeping transformation will be undergirded by support from grassroots mutual aid networks. Such efforts alone will not be enough to get us through the dangerous decades ahead, but they will help lay the foundation for more revolutionary change to come. Dean Spade, author of the book *Mutual Aid: Building Solidarity During This Crisis (And the Next)*, explains how mutual aid today connects to a better world tomorrow:

> I can imagine a world based on the principles of mutual aid in which everybody has what they need to survive, and people are working on reproducing the means of survival not because of a coercive system where they'll die or be criminalized if they don't have a wage job, but instead because of the pleasure of growing food that other people will eat, and making a sewer system that we're all using. People doing the work because they want everyone to have these things, not because if they didn't do that work, they would starve. A key piece is this deep desire to share well-being with all, and make sure everybody has what they need and nobody has a lot more than they need.[164]

Mutual aid societies of free and enslaved Black people formed during the late eighteenth and early nineteenth century in New York, Baltimore, Philadelphia, Boston, and Charleston. The Alianza Hispano-Americano, part of the *mutualista* movement organized in Tucson in the 1890s, persisted until the 1960s, with new chapters forming coast to coast. By that time, the United Farm Workers in California had become as much a mutual aid society as a union.[165] A half century later in 2020, Black Lives Matter in Houston was distributing food assistance and school supplies to Black families, while the chapter in Portland was providing food, diapers, portable toilets, KN95 masks, gloves, burn bandaging, and medical assistance to wildfire and smoke victims. Gas masks that had protected protesters from police tear gas over the summer were repurposed for smoke protection. One Portland mutual-aid activist told *Truthout*, "We are talking about defunding the police and we are building something to replace it with—to show people there are other models, where no one will fall through the cracks."[166]

Mutual aid's roots reach even farther back in time than the nineteenth century and far beyond our borders. Writing for *The Walrus* in Vancouver, Vicki Mochama has described how, when first the pandemic and then the George Floyd killing shook not just the United States but the world, British Columbia's Black community "did something that, for Black folks, is as old as time: They started a mutual-aid group."[167] The group raised funds to create a pandemic-time pool of money that had reached $20,000 prior to the killing of George Floyd and rocketed to $170,000 soon after. The purpose of the fund was simple: Any Black person in the province could apply for money to take care of their unmet needs. Priority went to those who had fallen through the cracks of the government's emergency-aid system. Such mutual-aid practices, writes Mochama, have a long, proud tradition in Black cultures worldwide:

> Depending on where you're from and who invited you in, the pools have different names: *sol* (Haiti), *susu* (Ghana), *box hand* (Guyana), *jama* (Kenya), *hagbad* (Somalia)…but the principle is almost universally the same—you get out what you put in. A typical arrangement might look like this: Ten women decide to each contribute $30 a month to a pool, and they each get their turn receiving money from the pool—a $300 cash injection when they do. What enslaved people in Haiti and elsewhere knew is not too distant from

the wisdom of Somali mothers and Grenadian aunties: If everyone gives, everyone gets....In the years after slavery was abolished, mutual-aid groups would work together to build wealth by pooling resources to buy tractors, land, and feed....Groups like the Depression-era People's Consumer Cooperative did the same in pursuit of economic equity.

An organizer of one such mutual-aid network in Toronto pointed out that beyond the money exchange, there is constant discussion among participants: "The goal is the talking, which builds trust and helps dispel trepidation about managing finances. Cooperative economics invests trust in people through time and conversation and sharing instead of through cash and credit."[168]

In 2016, the *American Journal of Public Health* celebrated the fiftieth anniversary of the formation of the Black Panther Party with a commentary by Mary T. Bassett, then the commissioner of the New York City Department of Health and Mental Hygiene. Dr. Bassett highlighted how, soon after their founding, the Panthers built upon their original mission—armed self-defense of the Black community against police violence—in order to mobilize against "a more ambitiously framed concept of violence" that included lack of access to housing, education, income, and health care. Based on the "radical idea that achieving health for all demands a more just and equitable world," the Panthers established more than a dozen free clinics across the United States. In the 1970s, Dr. Bassett was in charge of the Panthers' national sickle-cell anemia screening campaign. The medical establishment of the time had largely ignored the debilitating genetic disorder—one that primarily affected people of African descent—and the Panthers' mutual-aid program filled that gaping hole.[169]

Of the many projects that the Black Panthers called "programs for survival," the most widely hailed was Breakfast for Children, which provided hearty, hot breakfasts to 50,000 school children in more than forty inner cities, free of charge. The breakfast program deserved all the praise it received, but the group's ultimate goals were more expansive, according to Raj Patel, writing for the organization Food First in 2011. They included ending militarism and police brutality and securing "land, bread, housing, education, clothing, justice, peace, and people's community control of modern technology" for all. The prominent Black Panther Huey Newton stressed that programs providing health care and school breakfasts "satisfy the deep needs of the community, but they are not solutions to our problems. That is why we call them survival programs, meaning survival pending revolution."[170]

Amid the devastation left by Hurricane Maria, mutual-aid and political organizing efforts rooted in climate justice principles sprang up all over Puerto Rico. The Centros de Apoyo Mutuo (Centers for Mutual Aid), the Centro para el Desarrollo Político, Educativo y Cultural (Center for Political, Educational and Cultural Development, CDPEC), and other mutual-aid networks set up road-clearing brigades, health clinics, free community kitchens, meal-delivery systems, solidarity networks, communication webs, and community solar generation. The artist and activist Molly Crabapple wrote at the time, "Many of these groups honed their activist skills fighting the punishing austerity cuts that the U.S. imposed to address Puerto Rico's debt crisis."[171] Activism extended far beyond the storm's immediate aftermath. In July 2019, in the largest demonstrations ever seen on the island, tens of thousands took over central San Juan to demand the resignation of Governor Ricardo Rosselló. The groundswell had begun in response to leaked group-chat messages by Rosselló and other officials in which, among other outrages, they had joked sadistically about Maria's high death toll. The movement's targets multiplied to include the austerity committee that Congress had empowered to control the government's meager finances; the post-Maria shuttering of hundreds of schools; and the government's continuing weak response to Maria, especially the botched restoration of electric power. The protests forced Rosselló to resign.[172] By the time the Covid-19 pandemic hit Puerto Rico, CDPEC had established ten centers throughout the island, focusing on delivery of food and other essentials and "dealing with the same issues that we've always dealt with," cofounder Giovanni Roberto told PRI's *The World*. "The best way of helping people is with the perspective of dignity and solidarity—not charity," he said. "Mutual aid builds power from the bottom up."[173]

Back in 2011, the Occupy movement erupted in cities across the country, with mutual aid being one of their key practices, especially legal support for the more than 7,000 people swept up in arrests nationwide. When Superstorm Sandy struck in late 2012, Occupy swooped into hard-hit areas of New York and New Jersey immediately after the storm to distribute food, clothing, and bedding. Occupy Sandy also organized a ride-share pool, provided construction and medical teams, and, crucially, carried out the removal and remediation of the dangerous black mold that blossomed in homes after the floodwaters receded. Out of these efforts came longer-term mutual-aid projects, including community gardens, neighborhood cooperatives, tool lending, food pantries, clinics, and grants to hard-hit areas through participatory budgeting. Spinoff groups have continued the work in the years since and were ready to provide invaluable assistance and political action when Covid-19 hit. The New Jersey Organizing Project, for example, has been involved not only in pandemic assistance but also in flood relief, renewable energy development, rent assistance, mortgage forbearance, passage of a fair housing bill in the State Assembly, and affordability of prescription drugs.[174]

A network called Mutual Aid Disaster Relief, formed during the Hurricane Katrina calamity, has drawn inspiration from the Black Panthers and their self-help programs. Much of its activity is carried out by self-organizing working groups around the country. In 2020, groups responded to back-to-back hurricanes on the Gulf

Coast, wildfires on the West Coast, the powerful derecho storm that tore through Iowa, and the pandemic everywhere, arranging, they reported, "porch wifi programs, community fridges, tool lending libraries, d.i.y. handwashing stations, mask distributions...pantry food delivery programs, herbal medicine care packages, eviction defense crews, bail funds."[175]

Paula Austin, an assistant professor of history and African American studies at Boston University, told *HuffPost* in 2020 that with mutual aid networks, "we're working on the revolution, but while we're working on the revolution, we need food and we need housing, and we need education and health care. We need all these things that our federal government is not providing." During the intertwined disasters, she said, "We're seeing a kind of interracial, maybe even cross-class coalition building. And people thinking about, 'What are my personal resources and how can I use them to support other people, who I may or may not be an actual community with, during the pandemic?'"[176]

AND ENVIRONMENTAL JUSTICE FOR ALL

SINCE THE 1980S, the environmental justice movement has been fighting against the practice of locating power plants and other polluting industrial facilities in predominantly Black and Latino neighborhoods and on tribal lands. Environmental justice has also become an academic discipline and even achieved governmental recognition, being defined by the federal Environmental Protection Agency as "the fair treatment and meaningful involvement of all people regardless of race, color, national origin, or income with respect to the development, implementation, and enforcement of environmental laws, regulations, and policies." However, it is the long-running grassroots struggle for environmental justice that is increasingly being looked to as a model for taking down the fossil fuel industry and achieving climate justice.

The land of the Navajo Nation is rich in coal, oil, natural gas, and uranium. The bulk of what is pumped or mined is hauled away to provide energy elsewhere, but for forty-five years, a goodly portion of the coal was fed into the Navajo Generating Station, the largest coal-fired power plant in the West. Emissions from the plant, which was located within the borders of the Navajo Reservation, were linked to severe health problems, including high rates of premature birth and low birth weight, and high death rates from heart and lung diseases. Regarding this injustice, Kathleen Brosemer of Michigan Technological University wrote, "Navajo coal has produced power in Navajo country since 1973, and power transmission lines march across the 27,000-square-mile reservation, yet hogans (Navajo homes) are still without power. Navajo citizens, residents of the region where the power plants were built, suffer the health impacts of electricity production without reaping its benefits." Thirty percent of reservation residents have no electricity, and one-third have no running water.[177]

Thanks in part to dogged campaigns by local Navajo and multiracial environmental justice groups, including Diné C.A.R.E. (Citizens Against Ruining our Environment) and the Black Mesa Water Coalition, the Navajo Generating Station was permanently closed in 2019. After a three-year process of dismantling the plant and hauling away the dirty debris, the plan was to reseed the land on which the station stood with plant species used for making dyes, tea, and traditional medicines. Speaking for the Black Mesa Water Coalition, Marie Gladue said, "We need to heal from the wrongs of the past by returning to Diné traditional law, and prioritizing energy and water management policies that are in line with our values and virtues as stewards of the natural world."[178]

Dina Gilio-Whitaker, the author of *As Long as Grass Grows*, told *Earther*, "We have an entire body of law and a policy framework that have been built over almost a century that are about tribal self-determination." She noted that defending their land rights under the law has put Indigenous people in the forefront of the struggle against the fossil fuel giants:

> At Standing Rock, for example, had there been meaningful consultation and proper environmental impact statements done, we would have had a completely different outcome, I think. The reason the Dakota Access Pipeline went through unceded treaty lands of the Standing Rock Sioux was because it got rerouted away from a white community. So, had the legal system actually worked the way it was supposed to, Standing Rock would never have happened. That pipeline would have had to have gone somewhere else, and if white people didn't want it going through their communities, compromising their water, maybe it would not have happened at all. We can only speculate, and maybe that's wrong. But there would have been more resistance to it from populations beyond Indian Country. So, it really is about sovereignty and about how indigenous land stewardship has knowledge that can protect environments, if there's political will to abide by it.[179]

Since 1999, the Philadelphia-based Energy Justice Network has been successfully fighting to prevent construction of, or shut down, a wide range of polluting facilities, located mostly in the midst of marginalized communities: coal- and gas-fired power plants; ethanol biorefineries; incinerators burning biomass, tires, trash, and sewage sludge; natural gas–fracking fields; and dumping of rock and coal waste. They publish an eye-popping interactive map of all U.S. coal, gas, oil, nuclear, and biomass power plants, which can be searched by zip code.[180]

Cooperation Jackson, rooted in the Mississippi state capital's Black community, is an environmental justice cooperative, but it's a lot more than that. Its "Build and Fight Formula" includes mutual aid, food sovereignty, cooperative economics, community production, self-defense, people's assemblies, people's strikes, democratizing the economy, freeing land, and a just transition "to restore the balance of natural ecosystems and human relations." It aims for "development of the solidarity economy in Jackson, Mississippi, to advance the struggle for economic democracy as a prelude towards the democratic transition to eco-socialism."[181] The movement has supported local progressive candidates, created a network of cooperatives, launched a Human Rights Institute and the Fannie Lou Hamer Community Land Trust, and, in 2020, organized a "Community Production Mask Give Away + Buy In." Its People's Strikes include "mass, non-violent direct action conducted in a coordinated campaign." Its Autonomous People's Assemblies "are organized as expressions of participatory and direct democracy to help people and communities exercise self-determination over their lives and circumstances."

When a polar air mass evicted from its home by climate disruption slumped down into the United States in early 2021 and walloped the south central states with deadly blizzards, freezes, and power outages, the city of Jackson completely lost its water supply, and residents' taps did not yield potable water again for over a month. To address the water and sanitation crisis, Operation Jackson launched "autonomous relief efforts" including distribution of water, safety masks, and sanitizing supplies, especially for houseless residents, as well as "emergency preparedness training for freezes, tornados, hurricanes, and floods," along with emergency kits containing water filters and purification tablets, large water containers, solar lighting, sleeping bags, and tarps.[182]

Kali Akuno, a co-founder of Operation Jackson, explained in an April 2020 interview about the then-exploding pandemic:

[This] would be the perfect call to start building toward a
general strike in this country. Because the things that we
were seeing, like in [pre-pandemic] February, most folk just
shake it off, any notion that universal healthcare could be
a possibility. Now, that's like a basic demand. So, the situation has just elevated people's consciousness to a great
degree. And we were like, let's try to play a role, step into
their void. Let's not let the Right define what the feeling is,
we need to from the Left, try to define it....We're working
to start building levels of self-governance in our community.
To really balance out the system. That's ultimately what
we're trying to get through that. And eradicate it, no ands
ifs or buts. But easier said than done. We got to move millions of people to that program. So that's something that we
will keep pushing for on our end. Struggling for that clarity
and programmatic unity. It's going to take time.[183]

✳ ✳ ✳

LOCAL AND REGIONAL mobilization can and must coalesce into
national mobilization. That's what happened with the Black Lives
Matter movement and has begun happening with the climate justice
movement. Although the pandemic temporarily slowed momentum
on the latter while seemingly boosting the former, they both now
have majority support in public opinion. That has not yet translated
into national policies and priorities, but transformation could be
within reach sooner than it seems.

Research on social "intervention points" and "tipping points"
shows that if the share of a population that is committed, vocal,
and active in support of a sharp departure from established policies
grows beyond a relatively low threshold, in the vicinity of 25 percent,

that commitment can mobilize passive supporters as well, and then quickly sweep through the rest of the population; in the words of researchers, "apparently stable societal norms can be effectively overturned by the efforts of small but committed minorities."[184] If individuals and groups committed to climate action, economic justice, and an end to systemic racism continue growing in number, turning up the volume, and joining forces, we can reach that threshold, cross over, and begin building a new and just society together.

The struggles of 2017–2021 have awakened a new consciousness of possibility and transformation, but they have not bought us time. "A generation is on the move," says Nick Estes, and the movement for a livable future is being led by the "young, queer, Black, Indigenous, and militant." Racial justice and reparations can't wait. Ecological restoration can't wait. Nor can workers' rights, a just food system, or universal health care. We can no longer wait to cut off fossil fuels at the source. So many years have been lost that it's far from certain that we can turn off the tap in time to prevent calamity. The sooner we do, however, the larger the share of the Earth that will remain habitable, not just for humans, but for the web of life of which we are but one small part. "The human race is in the middle of an earth-shattering historical moment," writes Adrian Parr: "We are poised between needing to radically transform how we live and becoming extinct."[185] A just and livable future can be ours, but only if we organize, resist, imagine, and forge the path there together.

ENDNOTES

1   Sarah Kaplan, "Climate Change Is Also a Racial Justice Problem," *Washington Post*, June 29, 2020.

2   Nick Estes, "Biden Killed the Keystone Pipeline. Good, but He Doesn't Get a Climate Pass Just Yet," *Guardian*, January 28, 2021.

3   Zack Colman, "Environmental Groups' Greatest Obstacle May Not Be Republican Opposition," *Politico*, February 5, 2021.

4   "Activist Tamika Mallory's Speech Goes Viral: 'We Learned Violence from You!'," *TheGrio*, May 30, 2020, thegrio.com/2020/05/30/tamika-mallory-george-floyd-speech/.

5   Lois Beckett, "'The Past Is So Present': How White Mobs Once Killed American Democracy," *Guardian*, February 22, 2021.

6   Jessic Zhu, "Prison abolition, democracy and capitalism are interconnected, say Angela Davis and Astra Taylor," *Stanford Daily*, October 15, 2020, stanforddaily.com/2020/10/14/prison-abolition-democracy-and-capitalism-are-interconnected-say-angela-davis-and-astra-taylor/.

7   James Baldwin, *No Name in the Street* (New York: Vintage, 2007)

8   United Nations Environment Program, "Emissions Gap Report 2020," December 9, 2020, https://www.unep.org/emissions-gap-report-2020.

9   Alliance for Pandemic Preparedness, "Provisional Life Expectancy Estimates for January through June, 2020," University of Washington, February 19, 2021, depts.washington.edu/pandemicalliance/2021/02/19/provisional-life-expectancy-estimates-for-january-through-june-2020; Nina Lakhani, "Indigenous Americans Dying from Covid at Twice the Rate of White Americans," *Guardian*, February 4, 2021; Liz Crampton, "'There's Tremendous Fear': Farmworkers Face Vaccine Eligibility Woes," *Politico*, March 18, 2021.

10   Angelina Jolie, "A Conversation with Angelina Jolie and Ugandan Climate Activist Vanessa Nakate On the Urgency of Elevating African Voices in Climate Discussions," *Time*, July 9, 2020.

11   Katherine Bagley, "Connecting the Dots Between Environmental Injustice and the Coronavirus," *Yale E360*, May 7, 2020.

12   Larry Buchanan, Quoctrung Bui, and Jugal K. Patel, "Black Lives Matter May Be the Largest Movement in U.S. History," *New York Times*, July 3, 2020.

13   Erika Smith, "2020 Was the Year America Embraced Black Lives Matter as a Movement, Not Just a Moment," *Los Angeles Times*, December 6, 2020.

14   Adam Serwer, "The New Reconstruction," *The Atlantic*, October 2020.

15   Dhaval Dave, Andrew Friedson, Kyutaro Matsuzawa, Joseph Sabia, and Samuel Safford, "Black Lives Matter Protests, Social Distancing, and COVID-19." Working Paper No. w27408, National Bureau of Economic Research (2020), nber.org/papers/w27408.

16   Douglas Bernheim, Nina Buchmann, Zach Freitas-Groff, and Sebastian Otero, "The Effects of Large Group Meetings on the Spread of COVID-19: The Case of Trump Rallies," Working Paper No. 20-043, Stanford Institute for Economic Policy Research, October 30, 2020, siepr.stanford.edu/sites/default/files/publications/20-043.pdf; Erin Mansfield, Josh Salman, and Dinah Voyles Pulver, "Trump's Campaign Made Stops Nationwide. Coronavirus Cases Surged in His Wake in at Least Five Places," *USA Today*, October 23, 2020.

17   Ocean Robbins, "Making Food Accessible for All: An Interview with Leah Penniman of Soul Fire Farm," *Food Revolution Network*, July 29, 2020, foodrevolution.org/blog/leah-penniman-soul-fire-farm-interview/.

18   Christopher Tessum, Joshua Apte, Andrew Goodkind, et al., "Inequity in Consumption of Goods and Services Adds to Racial–Ethnic Disparities in Air Pollution Exposure," *Proceedings of the National Academy of Sciences* 116, (2019): 6001–06.

19   Jeremy Németh and Sarah Rowan, "Is Your Neighborhood Raising Your Coronavirus Risk? Redlining Decades Ago Set Communities Up for Greater Danger," *The Conversation*, May 26, 2020; Jeremy Hoffman, Vivek Shandas, and Nicholas Pendleton, "The Effects of Historical Housing Policies on Resident Exposure to Intra-Urban Heat: A Study of 108 US Urban Areas," *Climate* 8 (2020): 12.

20   Marina Borro, Paolo Di Girolamo, Giovanna Gentile, Ottavia De Luca, Robert Preissner, Adriano Marcolongo, Stefano Ferracuti, and Maurizio Simmaco, "Evidence-Based Considerations Exploring Relations Between SARS-Cov-2 Pandemic and Air Pollution: Involvement of PM2.5-Mediated

Up-Regulation of the Viral Receptor ACE-2," *International Journal of Environmental Research and Public Health* 17 (2020): 5573.

21   Jonathan Jay, Jacob Bor, Elaine Nsoesie, Sarah Lipson, DavidJones, Sandro Galea, and Julia Raifman, "Neighbourhood Income and Physical Distancing During the COVID-19 Pandemic in the United States," *Nature Human Behaviour* (2020): 1294–1302.

22   Steven Mufson, "U.S. Greenhouse Gas Emissions Set to Drop to Lowest Level in Three Decades," *Washington Post*, November 19, 2020; Doyle Rice, "UN report: Climate Change Continues 'Unabated' Despite COVID-19 Lockdowns," *USA Today*, September 10, 2020.

23   "Biden-Sanders Unity Task Force Recommendations: Combating the Climate Crisis and Pursuing Environmental Justice," joebiden.com/wp-content/uploads/2020/08/unity-task-force-recommendations.pdf

24   Matthew Ballew, Edward Maibach, John Kotcher, Parrish Bergquist, Seth Rosenthal, Jennifer Marlon, and Anthony Leiserowitz, "Which Racial/Ethnic Groups Care Most About Climate Change?," Yale Program on Climate Change Communication, April 16, 2020, climatecommunication.yale.edu/publications/race-and-climate-change.

25   Emily Holden and Oliver Milman, "Democratic Platform's Backtracking on Fossil Fuels Dismays Climate Activists," *The Guardian*, August 20, 2020.

26   Ayana Elizabeth Johnson, "I'm a Black Climate Expert. Racism Derails Our Efforts to Save the Planet," *Washington Post*, June 3, 2020.

27   Molly Kinder, Laura Stateler, and Julia Du, "Windfall Profits and Deadly Risks," Brookings Institution, November 20, 2020, brookings.edu/essay/windfall-profits-and-deadly-risks/.

28   Ibid.

29   Miriam Jordan, "Thousands of Farmworkers Are Prioritized for the Coronavirus Vaccine," *New York Times*, March 1, 2021.

30   Laura Reiley and Beth Reinhard, "Virus's Unseen Hot Zone: The American Farm," *Washington Post*, September 24, 2020.

31   Miriam Jordan, "Migrant Farmworkers Under Lockdown: 'You're Practically a Slave,'" *New York Times*, October 19, 2020.

32   Center on Budget and Policy Priorities, "House Relief Package Would Help Millions and Bolster the Economy," cbpp.org/research/poverty-and-inequality/house-relief-package-would-help-millions-and-bolster-the-economy.

33   Robbins, "Making Food."

34   Shima Hamidi, Sadegh Sabouri, and Reid Ewing, "Does Density Aggravate the COVID-19 Pandemic? Early Findings and Lessons for Planners," *Journal of the American Planning Association* 86 (2020): 495–509.

35   Jim Offner, "Packaging Sector Enjoys Growth during Pandemic," *The Packer*. February 12, 2021, thepacker.com/markets/marketing/ packaging-sector-enjoys-growth-during-pandemic.

36   Lidia Morawska and Donald Milton, "It Is Time to Address Airborne Transmission of COVID-19," *Clinical Infectious Disease* 6 (2020): ciaa939.

37   Leslie Dietz, Patrick Horve, David Coil, Mark Fretz, Jonathan Eisen, and Kevin Van Den Wymelenberg, "2019 Novel Coronavirus (COVID-19) Pandemic: Built Environment Considerations to Reduce Transmission," *Msystems* 5 (2020): e00245-20; G. Aernout Somsen, Cees van Rijn, Stefan Kooij, Reinout Bem, and Daniel Bonn, "Small Droplet Aerosols in Poorly Ventilated Spaces and SARS-Cov-2 Transmission," *The Lancet Respiratory Medicine* (2020) 8: 658–59; Lily Hospers, James Smallcombe, Nathan Morris, Anthony Capon, and Ollie Jay, "Electric Fans: A Potential Stay-at-Home Cooling Strategy During the COVID-19 Pandemic This Summer?," *Science of the Total Environment* 747 (2020): 141–80.

38   Eileen Guo, "He Started a Covid-19 Vaccine Company. Then He Hosted a Superspreader Event," *MIT Technology Review*, technologyreview. com/2021/02/13/1018374/peter-diamandis-covid-superspreader-a360-confer- ence/; Jacey Fortin, "Technology Executive Apologizes After Dozens of Event Attendees Contract Covid-19," *New York Times*, February 16, 2021.

39   Reed Albergotti, "Rarefied Air: Taking a Healthy Breath Is Now a Luxury in California," *Washington Post*, September 18, 2020.

40   Ibid.

41   John Barry, *The Great Influenza: The Story of the Greatest Pandemic in History* (New York: Penguin, 2018), 339–41, 352–53, 460–61.

42   David Nakamura, "'Nobody Came, Nobody Helped': Fears of Anti- Asian Violence Rattle the Community," *Washington Post*, February 22, 2021; Christine Chung, "Anti-Asian Hate Crime Surge Fuels Demands for Systemic and Sensitive Responses," *The City*, February 11, 2021, thecity. nyc/2021/2/11/22279407/anti-asian-hate-crime-surge-fuels-demands-for- systemic-and-sensitive-responses; Moriah Balingit, Hannah Natanson, and Yutao Chen, "As Schools Reopen, Asian American Students Are Missing from Classrooms," *Washington Post*, March 4, 2021.

43   Miranda Bryant, "Atlanta Spa Shootings: US on Alert over Possible Anti- Asian American Motive," *Guardian*, March 17, 2021; Jon Alsop, "Hesitant Coverage of the Hateful Atlanta Shootings," *Columbia Journalism Review*,

March 19, 2021, cjr.org/the_media_today/atlanta_shootings_media_hate_
crime.php

44   Tim Elfrink, "Trevor Noah Slams Claim That Racism Didn't Motivate
Atlanta Shootings: 'Your Murders Speak Louder than Your Words,'"
Washington Post, March 18, 2021.

45   David Wallace-Wells, "How the West Lost COVID," *New York
Magazine*, March 15, 2021.

46   Subhabrata Bobby Banerjee, John Jermier, Ana Maria Peredo, Robert
Perey, and André Reichel, "Theoretical Perspectives on Organizations and
Organizing in a Post-Growth Era," *Organization* (2020): 1350508420973629.

47   On silver linings and wakeup calls in time of disaster, see Stan Cox
and Paul Cox, *How the World Breaks: Life in Catastrophe's Path, from the
Caribbean to Siberia* (New York: The New Press, 2016), 88–121.

48   "Martin Luther King Jr: 'It Really Boils Down to This: That All
Life Is Interrelated,' Interconnected World Sermon," December 24, 1967,
Ebenezer Baptist Church, Atlanta, Georgia, undated, speakola.com/ideas/
martin-luther-king-jr-interconnected-world-massey-5-1967.

49   Benjamin Sovacool, Dylan Furszyfer Del Rio, and Steve Griffiths,
"Contextualizing the Covid-19 Pandemic for a Carbon-Constrained
World: Insights for Sustainability Transitions, Energy Justice, and Research
Methodology," *Energy Research & Social Science* 68 (2020): 101701.

50   Adrian Parr (interviewed by Natasha Lennard), "Our Crime Against the
Planet, and Ourselves," *New York Times*, May 18, 2016

51   Julia Steinberger, "Pandenomics: A Story of Life Versus Growth,"
Open Democracy, April 8, 2020, opendemocracy.net/en/oureconomy/
pandenomics-story-life-versus-growth.

52   David Morens, Joel Breman, Charles Calisher, Peter Doherty, Beatrice
Hahn, Gerald Keusch, Laura Kramer, James LeDuc, Thomas Monath, and Jeffery
Taubenberger, "The Origin of COVID-19 and Why It Matters," *American Journal
of Tropical Medicine and Hygiene* 103 (2020): 955–59.

53   Jacob Kushner, "Why Camels Are Worrying Coronavirus Hunters," *BBC*,
January 26, 2021, bbc.com/future/article/20210122-the-coronavirus-10-times-
more-deadly-than-covid.

54   Morens et al., "Origin"; Stephen Goldstein, et al., "Extensive
Recombination-Driven Coronavirus Diversification Expands the Pool of Potential
Pandemic Pathogens," *bioRxiv* (2021): doi.org/10.1101/2021.02.03.429646.

55   David Morens and Anthony Fauci, "Emerging Pandemic Diseases: How
We Got to COVID-19," *Cell* 182 (2020): 1077–92.

56   Intergovernmental Panel on Climate Change, *Global Warming of 1.5° C*, October 2018, www.ipcc.ch/sr15.

57   Abrahm Lustgarten, "Climate Change Will Force a New American Migration," *ProPublica*, September 15, 2020.

58   Nadege Green, "As Miami Faces Threats from Sea Level Rise, Some Worry About Climate Gentrification," *NPR*, December 2, 2020, npr. org/2019/12/02/784225385/as-miami-faces-threats-from-sea-level-rise-some-worry-about-climate-gentrificati.

59   Jeremy Deaton, "The Scariest Thing about Climate Change Isn't the Weather—It's Us," *Fast Company*, February 9, 2021.

60   Chi Xu, Timothy Kohler, Timothy Lenton, Jens-Christian Svenning, and Marten Scheffer, "Future of the Human Climate Niche," *Proceedings of the National Academy of Sciences* 117 (2020): 11350–355.

61   Narasimha Rao and Jihoon Min, "Decent Living Standards: Material Prerequisites for Human Wellbeing," *Social Indicators Research* 138 (2018): 225–44.

62   Joel Millward-Hopkins, Julia Steinberger, Narasimha Rao, and Yannick Oswald, "Providing Decent Living with Minimum Energy: A Global Scenario," *Global Environmental Change* 65 (2020): 102168.

63   Ryan Finnigan and Kelsey Meagher, "Past Due: Combinations of Utility and Housing Hardship in the United States," *Sociological Perspectives* 62 (2019): 96–119.

64   Deborah Sunter, Sergio Castellanos, and Daniel Kammen, "Disparities in Rooftop Photovoltaics Deployment in the United States by Race and Ethnicity," *Nature Sustainability* 2 (2019): 71–76.

65   Kelsey Misbrener, "Installers Must Act Now to Resolve Racial Disparity in Rooftop Solar," *Solar Power World*, July 23, 2019, solarpowerworldonline. com/2019/07/installers-racial-disparity-rooftop-solar.

66   Sunter et al., "Disparities"

67   Emily Hazzard, "A Conversation with Wes Jackson, President of the Land Institute," *The Atlantic*, March 23, 2011.

68   Leah Penniman, "What Does an Ecological Civilization Look Like?" *YES! Magazine*, February 16, 2021.

69   Michael Perelman, *The Perverse Economy* (New York: Palgrave Macmillan, 2003), 11–13.

70   John R. Schramski, C. Brock Woodson, and James H. Brown. "Energy Use and the Sustainability of Intensifying Food Production," *Nature Sustainability* 3 (2020): 257–59.

71   Corey Bradshaw, Paul Ehrlich, Andrew Beattie, et al., "Underestimating the Challenges of Avoiding a Ghastly Future," *Frontiers in Conservation Science* 1 (2021): 615419.

72   Food and Agriculture Organization, "Livestock a Major Threat to Environment," November 6, 2006, fao.org/newsroom/en/news/2006/1000448/index.html.

73   International Energy Agency, "Net Zero by 2050: A Roadmap for the Global Energy Sector," May 18, 2021, iea.blob.core.windows.net/assets/0716bb9a-6138-4918-8023-cb24caa47794/NetZeroby2050-ARoadmapfortheGlobalEnergySector.pdf

74   See Stan Cox, *The Green New Deal and Beyond: Ending the Climate Emergency While We Still Can* (San Francisco: City Lights, 2020) for a review of faulty research purporting to show that a high-energy society can be sustained using 100 percent renewable energy.

75   Joshua Floyd, Samuel Alexander, Manfred Lenzen, Patrick Moriarty, Graham Palmer, Sangeetha Chandra-Shekeran, Barney Foran, and Lorenz Keyßer, "Energy Descent as a Post-Carbon Transition Scenario: How 'Knowledge Humility' Reshapes Energy Futures for Post-Normal Times," *Futures* 122 (2020): 102565.

76   Janice Lee, "An Interview with Robin Wall Kimmerer," *Believer*, November 3, 2020.

77   Schramski et al., "Energy Use."

78   Allison Keyes, "Gullah-Geechee Community: Hear Us on Climate Change," *The Root*, May 29, 2019.

79   Cameron Hepburn, Brian O'Callaghan, Nicholas Stern, Joseph Stiglitz, and Dimitri Zenghelis. "Will COVID-19 Fiscal Recovery Packages Accelerate or Retard Progress on Climate Change?," *Oxford Review of Economic Policy* 36 (2020): S359-81.

80   Marie Patino, "A New Survey of New Yorkers Exposes Pandemic Inequality," *Bloomberg*, February 24, 2021.

81   Amanda Cooper, "U.S. Billionaires Saw Their Net Worth Rise by Almost $1 Trillion Between March and October—Jeff Bezos Remains the Richest, a Study Says," *Business Insider Australia*, October 20, 2020.

82   Ed Pilkington, "As 100,000 Die, the Virus Lays Bare America's Brutal Fault Lines—Race, Gender, Poverty and Broken Politics," *Guardian*, May 28, 2020.

83   "Fossil Fuel Shock Doctrine: Naomi Klein on Deadly Deregulation & Why Texas Needs the Green New Deal," *Democracy Now!*, February 22, 2021.

84   T. Wiedmann, M. Lenzen, L.T. Keyßer, and J.K. Steinberger, "Scientists' Warning on Affluence," *Nature Communications* 11 (2020): 1–10.

85   Alex de Vries, "Bitcoin Boom: What Rising Prices Mean for the Network's Energy Consumption," *Joule* 5 (2021): 509–13.

86   Logan Kugler, "Why Cryptocurrencies Use So Much Energy and What to Do About It," *Communications of the ACM* 61 (2018): 15–17.

87   Nick Rose, "Bitcoin Is a Pyramid Scheme, Economist Says," *Yahoo! Finance*, January 1, 2020, finance.yahoo.com/news/economist-bitcoin-is-a-pyramid-scheme-204217615.html.

88   Andrew Ross Sorkin, "Bitcoin's Climate Problem," *New York Times,* March 9, 2021; www.nytimes.com/2021/03/09/business/dealbook/bitcoin-climate-change.html.

89   Daniel Horen Greenford, Timothy Crownshaw, Corey Lesk, Konstantin Stadler, and Damon Matthews, "Shifting Economic Activity to Services Has Limited Potential to Reduce Global Environmental Impacts Due to the Household Consumption of Labour," *Environmental Research Letters* 15 (2020): 064019.

90   Aubrey Streit Krug, "Ecospheric Care Work," *The Ecological Citizen* 3 (2020): 143–48.

91   "ICA Youth Delegation Demand Non-Market Climate Solutions and Indigenous Rights in Article 6," Indigenous Climate Action, December 5, 2019, www.indigenousclimateaction.com/post/ica-youth-delegation-demand-non-market-climate-solutions-and-indigenous-rights-in-article-6.

92   Mark Paul, Carla Santos Skandier, and Rory Renzy, "Out of Time: The Case for Nationalizing the Fossil Fuel Industry," The Democracy Collaborative, June 2020, thenextsystem.org/learn/stories/out-time-case-nationalizing-fossil-fuel-industry.

93   Justin Gillis and Michael O'Boyle, "When Will Electricity Companies Finally Quit Natural Gas?," *New York Times*, November 12, 2020.

94   Herman Daly, *Beyond Growth: The Economics of Sustainable Development* (Boston: Beacon, 1996), 52–57.

95   Ezra Silk and Kaela Bamberger, *The Climate Mobilization Victory Plan*, The Climate Mobilization, March 2019, theclimatemobilization.org/victory-plan; Larry Edwards and Stan Cox: "Cap and Adapt: Failsafe Policy for the Climate Emergency," *Solutions* 11 (2020): 22–31.

96   Elinor Ostrom, "Beyond Markets and States: Polycentric Governance of Complex Economic Systems," *American Economic Review* 100 (2010): 641–72.

97   For more on the following examples and others, see Johanna Bozuwa, Matthew Burke, Stan Cox, and Carla Skandier, "Re-Imagining Democratic Governance for the Decline of Fossil Fuels," in *Democratizing Energy: Imaginaries, Transitions, Risks*, Majia Nadesan, Jennifer Keahey, and Martin Pasqualetti (eds.) (New York: Elsevier, 2021), in press.

98   Rebecca Abers, "Learning Democratic Practice: Distributing Government Resources through Popular Participation in Porto Alegre, Brazil," in *The Challenge of Urban Government Policies and Practices*, Mila Freire and Richard Stren (eds.) (Washington: The World Bank Institute, 2001).

99   Martin Calisto Friant, "Deliberating for Sustainability: Lessons from the Porto Alegre Experiment with Participatory Budgeting," *International Journal of Urban Sustainable Development* 11 (2019): 81–99.

100   David Zahniser and Dakota Smith, "Black Lives Matter Leaders Meet with L.A. Politicians, Saying 'Defund the Police,'" *Los Angeles Times*, June 15, 2020; Black Lives Matter Los Angeles, "The People's Budget," undated, peoplesbudgetla.com/peoplesbudget/.

101   Brittany Martin, "A Look at the 'People's Budget' L.A. Activists Are Promoting," *Los Angeles Magazine*, June 2, 2020.

102   Felicia Sonmez and Colby Itkowitz, "House Passes Expansive Policing Overhaul Bill Named in Honor of George Floyd," *Washington Post*, March 3, 2021.

103   Zack Linly, "The Movement for Black Lives Opposes the George Floyd Justice in Policing Act. Here's Why the Movement Has a Point," *The Root*, March 17, 2021.

104   Jessica Blatt Press, "Citizens' Assemblies," *Philadelphia Citizen*, Oct. 19, 2020, thephiladelphiacitizen.org/citizens-assemblies.

105   Justin Kenrick, "If Citizens Assemblies Are the Way Forward, Why Is XR No Longer Endorsing the Scottish Governments Climate Citizens Assembly?," *Bella Caledonia*, November 4, 2020, bellacaledonia.org.uk/2020/11/04/if-citizens-assemblies-are-the-way-forward-why-is-xr-no-longer-endorsing-the-scottish-governments-climate-citizens-assembly.

106 Jess Phelps, "A Vision of the New Deal Unfulfilled—Soil and Water Conservation Districts and Land Use Regulation," *Drake Journal of Agricultural Law* 11 (2006): 353–81.

107 Don Fitz, *Cuban Health Care: The Ongoing Revolution* (New York: Monthly Review Press, 2019), 244–56.

108 Reuben Oppenheimer, "The War Price and Rationing Boards. An Experiment in Decentralization," *Columbia Law Review* 43 (1943): 147–64.

109 Phelps, "A Vision."

110 Efraín O'Neill-Carrillo and Agustín Irizarry-Rivera, "How to Harden Puerto Rico's Grid Against Hurricanes," *IEEE Spectrum* 56 (2019): 42–48.

111 Peter Newell and Andrew Simms, "Towards a Fossil Fuel Non-Proliferation Treaty," *Climate Policy* 20 (2020): 1043–54.

112 "101 Nobel Laureates Urge World Leaders to Keep Fossil Fuels in the Ground," April 21, 2021, fossilfueltreaty.org/nobel-letter.

113 Newell and Simms, "Towards a Fossil Fuel."

114 Greg Muttitt and Sivan Kartha, "Equity, Climate Justice and Fossil Fuel Extraction: Principles for a Managed Phase Out," *Climate Policy* (2020): 1–19.

115 Lily Hospers, James Smallcombe, Nathan Morris, Anthony Capon, and Ollie Jay, "Electric Fans: A Potential Stay-at-Home Cooling Strategy During the COVID-19 Pandemic this Summer?," *Science of the Total Environment* 747 (2020): 141180.

116 Kurt Waldman, David Conner, Adam Montri, Michael Hamm, and John Biernbaum, "Hoophouse Farming Startup: Economics, Efforts, and Experiences from 12 Novice Hoophouse Farmers," *Extension Bulletin* 3138, Michigan State University, December, 2010, canr.msu.edu/uploads/resources/pdfs/hoophouse_farming_startup_(e3138).pdf.

117 Katrina Quisumbing King, Spencer Wood, Jess Gilbert, and Marilyn Sinkewicz, "Black Agrarianism: The Significance of African American Landownership in the Rural South," *Rural Sociology* 83 (2018): 677–99; Dorceta Taylor, "Black Farmers in the USA and Michigan: Longevity, Empowerment, and Food Sovereignty," *Journal of African American Studies* 22 (2018): 49–76.

118 Taylor, "Black Farmers"

119 King et al., "Black Agrarianism."

120 Taylor, "Black Farmers."

121 Soul Fire Farm, "Take Action," undated, soulfirefarm.org/get-involved/
take-action; Soul Fire Farm, "Reparations," undated, soulfirefarm.org/
get-involved/reparations.

122 Ocean Robbins, "Making Food Accessible for All: An Interview with
Leah Penniman of Soul Fire Farm," *Food Revolution Network*, July 29, 2020,
foodrevolution.org/blog/leah-penniman-soul-fire-farm-interview/.

123 Adam Boffa, "'We Are Nations:' What Environmental Justice Looks Like
for Indigenous People," *Earther*, October 19, 2019, earther.gizmodo.com/
we-are-nations-what-environmental-justice-looks-like-f-1839028507.

124 Laura-Anne Minkoff-Zern, "Race, Immigration and the Agrarian
Question: Farmworkers Becoming Farmers in the United States," *Journal of
Peasant Studies* 45 (2018): 389–408.

125 Laura-Anne Minkoff-Zern and Sea Sloat, "A New Era of Civil Rights?
Latino Immigrant Farmers and Exclusion at the United States Department of
Agriculture," *Agriculture and Human Values* 34 (2017): 631–43.

126 Minkoff-Zern, "Race."

127 Queen Quet, "Support Gullah/Geechee Rising SEA and Help
#GullahGeechee Resiliency," Gulla/Geechee Nation (blog), September 1, 2019,
gullahgeecheenation.com/2019/09/01/support-gullah-geechee-rising-sea-and-
help-gullahgeechee-resiliency.

128 Adeline Chen and Teo Kermeliotis, "African Slave Traditions Live on in
U.S.," *CNN*, May 25, 2018; Queen Quet, "Support"; Brentin Mock, "150
Hurricanes Later, These Island People Can Teach Us a Few Things about
Surviving Climate Change," *Grist*, September 30, 2014.

129 Mock, "150 Hurricanes."

130 Ibid.; Allison Keyes, "Gullah-Geechee Community: Hear Us On Climate
Change," *The Root*, May 29, 2019.

131 Wes Jackson and Robert Jensen, "Let's Get 'Creaturely': A New
Worldview Can Help Us Face Ecological Crises," *Resilience*, April 3, 2019,
resilience.org/stories/2019-04-03/lets-get-creaturely-a-new-worldview-can-help-
us-face-ecological-crises

132 G.P. Moreda, M.A. Muñoz-García, and P.J.E.C. Barreiro, "High Voltage
Electrification of Tractor and Agricultural Machinery—A Review," *Energy
Conversion and Management* 115 (2016): 117–31.

133 John Schramski, C. Brock Woodson, and James Brown, "Energy Use and
the Sustainability of Intensifying Food Production," *Nature Sustainability* 3
(2020): 257–59.

134   Timothy Crews, "Closing the Gap between Grasslands and Grain Agriculture," *Kansas Journal of Law and Public Policy* 26 (2016): 274–96.

135   Aubrey Streit Krug and Omar Imseeh Tesdell, "A Social Perennial Vision: Transdisciplinary Inquiry for the Future of Diverse, Perennial Grain Agriculture," *Plants, People, Planet*, doi.org/10.1002/ppp3.10175.

136   Ibid.

137   Laura Reiley, "Relief Bill Is Most Significant Legislation for Black Farmers since Civil Rights Act, Experts Say," *Washington Post*, March 8, 2021.

138   Leah Penniman, *Farming While Black: Soul Fire Farm's Practical Guide to Liberation on the Land* (White River Junction, VT: Chelsea Green, 2018), 3.

139   Dayna Scott and Adrian Smith, "'Sacrifice Zones' in the Green Energy Economy: Toward an Environmental Justice Framework," *McGill Law Journal* 62 (2017): 861–98.

140   Max Ajl, "Andreas Malm's *Corona, Climate, Chronic Emergency*," *Brooklyn Rail*, November 2020, brooklynrail.org/2020/11/field-notes/Corona-Climate-Chronic-Emergency.

141   Amartya Sen and Jean Drèze, *Hunger and Public Action* (Oxford: Oxford University Press, 1991), 13.

142   Janice Lee, "An Interview with Robin Wall Kimmerer," *Believer*, November 3, 2020.

143   Joshua Floyd, Samuel Alexander, Manfred Lenzen, Patrick Moriarty, Graham Palmer, Sangeetha Chandra-Shekeran, Barney Foran, and Lorenz Keyßer, "Energy Descent as a Post-Carbon Transition Scenario: How 'Knowledge Humility' Reshapes Energy Futures for Post-Normal Times," *Futures* 122 (2020): 102565.

144   See, for example, Elaine Godfrey, "Vaccine Hesitancy Could Create COVID Islands," *The Atlantic*, April 14, 2021.

145   Efraín O'Neill-Carrillo and Agustín Irizarry-Rivera, "How to Harden Puerto Rico's Grid Against Hurricanes," *IEEE Spectrum* 56 (2019): 42–48; Jennifer Hinojosa and Edwin Meléndez, "The Housing Crisis in Puerto Rico and the Impact of Hurricane Maria," Centro de Estudios Puertorriqueños, Hunter College (2018), centropr.hunter.cuny.edu/sites/default/files/data_briefs/HousingPuertoRico.pdf; Ivelisse Rivera Quiñones, "Sheet Roofs: Puerto Rico Reels 2 Years After Hurricane Maria," *Phys.org*, September 20, 2019, phys.org/news/2019-09-sheet-roofs-puerto-rico-reels.html.

146   John Romankiewicz, Cara Bottorff, and Leah Stokes, "The Dirty Truth About Utility Climate Pledges," Sierra Club, 2020, coal.sierraclub.org/the-problem/dirty-truth-greenwashing-utilities.

147 Hazel Sheffield, "'Carbon-Neutrality Is a Fairy Tale: How the Race for Renewables Is Burning Europe's Forests," *Guardian*, January 14, 2021.

148 Martin Cames et al., "How Additional Is the Clean Development Mechanism?," Oeko-Institut EV ClIMA. B 3 (2016), verifavia.com/uploads/files/clean_dev_mechanism_en.pdf.

149 James Temple, "Carbon Farming Is Raising a Lot of Climate Hopes—and a Lot of Concerns," *MIT Technology Review*, June 3, 2020; June Sekera and Andreas Lichtenberger, "Assessing Carbon Capture: Public Policy, Science, and Societal Need," *Biophysical Economics and Sustainability* 5 (2020): 14–28. For more on carbon capture, see Cox, *The Green New Deal and Beyond*, 64–65.

150 Cox, *The Green New Deal and Beyond*, 109–110.

151 Maya King, "Inside Black Lives Matter's Push for Power," *Politico*, November 17, 2020.

152 Cara Daggett, "Petro-Masculinity: Fossil Fuels and Authoritarian Desire," *Millennium* 47 (2018): 25–44.

153 John Asafu-Adjaye et al., "An Ecomodernist Manifesto," April 2015, eco-modernism.org.

154 Cox, *The Green New Deal and Beyond*, 84–85.

155 Brandi Morris, Polymeros Chrysochou, Simon T. Karg, and Panagiotis Mitkidis, "Optimistic vs. Pessimistic Endings in Climate Change Appeals," *Humanities and Social Sciences Communications* 7 (2020): 1–8; Matthew Hornsey and Kelly Fielding, "A Cautionary Note about Messages of Hope: Focusing on Progress in Reducing Carbon Emissions Weakens Mitigation Motivation," *Global Environmental Change* 39 (2016): 26–34.

156 The Dark Mountain Project, "Uncivilisation: The Dark Mountain Manifesto," undated, dark-mountain.net/about/manifesto/ (converted to U.S. English spelling).

157 Timothée Parrique, *The Political Economy of Degrowth*, Ph.D. dissertation, Stockholm University, 2019, ffNNT: 2019CLFAD003ff. fftel-02499463ff, theses.fr/2019CLFAD003.

158 Riccardo Mastini, Giorgos Kallis, and Jason Hickel, "A Green New Deal Without Growth?" *Ecological Economics* 179 (2021): 106832; Giorgos Kallis, *Degrowth* (Newcastle-upon-Tyne: Agenda, 2018); Julia Steinberger, "Pandenomics: A Story of Life Versus Growth," *Open Democracy*, April 8, 2020, opendemocracy.net/en/oureconomy/pandenomics-story-life-versus-growth; Jason Hickel and Giorgos Kallis; "Is Green Growth Possible?," *New Political Economy* 25 (2020): 469–86.

159 Parrique kindly acknowledges that he borrowed the slogan "sufficiency for all, excess for none" from Stan Cox, "That Green Growth at the Heart of the Green New Deal? It's Malignant," *Green Social Thought*, January 15, 2019, resilience.org/stories/2019-01-15/that-green-growth-at-the-heart-of-the-green-new-deal-its-malignant.

160 Mohamed Younis, "Four in 10 Americans Embrace Some Form of Socialism," Gallup.com, May 20, 2019, news.gallup.com/poll/257639/four-americans-embrace-form-socialism.aspx.

161 Rachel Cohen, "The Coronavirus Made the Radical Possible," *New York Times*, March 11, 2021.

162 Alicia Garza, *The Purpose of Power: How We Come Together When We Fall Apart*, (New York: One World/Penguin Random House, 2020), 147–48.

163 Ibid, 1.

164 Clara Liang, "Dean Spade on How Mutual Aid Will Help Us Survive Disaster," *In These Times*, November 20, 2020.

165 Amanda Schupak, "Behind America's Mutual Aid Boom Lies a Long History of Government Neglect," *HuffPost*, July 2, 2020.

166 Simon Davis-Cohen, "Mutual Aid Response During Fires Shows Black Lives Matter Is Building Community," *Truthout*, September 18, 2020.

167 Vicky Mochama, "Black Communities Have Known about Mutual Aid All Along," *The Walrus*, September 1, 2020, thewalrus.ca/black-communities-have-known-about-mutual-aid-all-along.

168 Ibid.

169 Mary T. Bassett, "Beyond Berets: The Black Panthers as Health Activists," *American Journal of Public Health* 106 (2016): 1741–43.

170 Raj Patel, "Survival Pending Revolution: What the Black Panthers Can Teach the US Food Movement," 115–37, in Samir Amin, Raj Patel, and Eric Holt-Giménez, *Food Movements Unite!: Strategies to Transform Our Food Systems* (Oakland, CA: Food First Books, 2011).

171 Molly Crabapple, "Puerto Rico's DIY Disaster Relief," *New York Review of Books*, November 17, 2017.

172 Michael Weissenstein, "Puerto Ricans Try to Forge Movement to Oust Governor," Associated Press, July 18, 2019; Marisa Gerber and Milton Carrero Galarza, "Puerto Rico Gov. Ricardo Rossello Announces Resignation amid Mounting Protests," *Los Angeles Times*, July 25, 2019.

173 Anna Kusmer, "Mutual Aid Groups Respond to Double Threat of Coronavirus and Climate Change," *The World*, April 13, 2020, pri.org/

stories/2020-04-13/mutual-aid-groups-respond-double-threat-coronavirus-and-climate-change.

174 See newjerseyop.org.

175 Mutual Aid Disaster Relief, "The Future Is Now: Overlapping Constant Disaster and Mutual Aid as Survival Strategy," October 5, 2020, mutualaiddisasterrelief.org/the-future-is-now-overlapping-constant-disaster-and-mutual-aid-as-survival-strategy.

176 Schupak, "Behind America's Mutual Aid Pact."

177 Kathleen Brosemer, Chelsea Schelly, Valoree Gagnon, Kristin Arola, Joshua Pearce, Douglas Bessette, and Laura Schmitt Olabisi, "The Energy Crises Revealed by COVID: Intersections of Indigeneity, Inequity, and Health," *Energy Research & Social Science* 68 (2020): 101661.

178 Felicia Fonseca, "Long-Running Coal Plant on Navajo Nation Stops Production," Associated Press, November 18, 2019.

179 Adam Boffa, "'We Are Nations': What Environmental Justice Looks Like for Indigenous People," *Earther*, October 19, 2019, earther.gizmodo.com/we-are-nations-what-environmental-justice-looks-like-f-1839028507.

180 See energyjustice.net/map.

181 See cooperationjackson.org.

182 Ibid.

183 Marisa Miale, "Toward the Mass Strike: Interview with Two Southern Organizers," *Cosmonaut*, April 29, 2020, cosmonaut.blog/2020/04/29/toward-the-mass-strike-interview-with-two-southern-organizers.

184 Damon Centola, Joshua Becker, Devon Brackbill, and Andrea Baronchelli, "Experimental Evidence for Tipping Points in Social Convention," *Science* 360 (2018): 1116–19.

185 Adrian Parr, *The Wrath of Capital: Neoliberalism and Climate Change Politics* (New York: Columbia University Press, 2013) 3.

ACKNOWLEDGMENTS

I COULD NOT have written this book in isolation through the depths of pandemic-time without the support, encouragement, and love of my family, including Priti Gulati Cox, Sheila Cox, Paul Cox, and Brenda Cox. This book's big idea was suggested by Greg Ruggiero of City Lights, and his inspired suggestions were essential to creating the book you see here. Finally, my deepest gratitude goes out to everyone out there who is on the front lines every day creating a future for racial justice, workers' rights, Indigenous sovereignty, sufficiency and equality for all, ecological sanity, and all the other essential elements of a livable future.

ABOUT THE AUTHOR

S TAN COX BEGAN HIS career in the U.S. Department of Agriculture and is now a research scholar in Ecosphere Studies at The Land Institute. Cox is the author of *The Green New Deal and Beyond: Ending the Climate Emergency While We Still Can*; *Any Way You Slice It: The Past, Present, and Future of Rationing*, and *Losing Our Cool: Uncomfortable Truths About Our Air-Conditioned World (and Finding New Ways to Get Through the Summer)*; he is co-author, with Paul Cox, of *How the World Breaks: Life in Catastrophe's Path, from the Carribbean to Siberia*. His writings on the economic and political roots of the global ecological crisis have appeared in the *New York Times, Washington Post, Los Angeles Times, Hartford Courant, Atlanta Journal-Constitution, Baltimore Sun, Denver Post, Kansas City Star, Arizona Republic, The New Republic, The Guardian, Al Jazeera, Salon,* and *Dissent,* and in local publications spanning forty-three U.S. states. In 2012, *The Atlantic* declared Cox the magazine's "Readers' Choice Brave Thinker" for his critique of air conditioning. He is based in Salina, Kansas.